Amadeus
A Mozart Mosaic

BOOKS BY HERBERT KUPFERBERG

Those Fabulous Philadelphians: The Life and Times of a Great Orchestra
The Mendelssohns: Three Generations of Genius
Opera (World of Culture series)
Tanglewood
The Raised Curtain (Report of the Twentieth Century Fund Task
    Force on Soviet-American Scholarly and Cultural Exchanges)
Basically Bach
The Book of Classical Music Lists

Juveniles

Felix Mendelssohn: His Life, His Family, His Music
A Rainbow of Sound: The Instruments of the Orchestra and Their Music

Amadeus
A Mozart Mosaic

HERBERT KUPFERBERG

McGRAW-HILL BOOK COMPANY

New York St. Louis San Francisco
Toronto Hamburg Mexico

1 2 3 4 5 6 7 8 9 F G R F G R 8 7 6

ISBN 0-07-035664-5

LIBRARY OF CONGRESS CATALOGING-IN-PUBLICATION DATA

Kupferberg, Herbert.
   Amadeus : a Mozart mosaic.
   Includes index.
   1. Mozart, Wolfgang Amadeus, 1756–1791.   2. Composers—
Austria—Biography.   3. Mozart, Wolfgang Amadeus,
1756–1791—Addresses, essays, lectures.   I. Title.
ML410.M9K96   1986   780′.92′4 [B]   85-31044
ISBN 0-07-035664-5

BOOK DESIGN BY PATRICE FODERO

To Barbara

Mann und Weib, und Weib und Mann
Reichen an die Gottheit an.

—THE MAGIC FLUTE

Contents

CONTENTS

Preface

Although the man and his music are inseparable, this book is more about Mozart the human being than it is about Mozart the composer. His life story has had endless retellings not only by biographers but by novelists, romancers, playwrights, and, most recently, moviemakers. Yet it seemed to me that there might be a place for one more book about him, written from a perspective somewhat different from most others.

Rather than following the customary chronological order, I have tried to recount Mozart's life and achievements in terms of his relationships with his family, his friends, his enemies, his patrons, his physicians, his audiences, even his pets. Mozart was no lonely genius; he constantly interacted with the busy, changing society around him. Virtually everything he did was in relation to something or somebody else.

This book explores those relationships, as reflected in such somewhat unusual chapter headings as "The Prodigy Market," "Mozart and Paris," "The Fiscal Mozart," "Mozart's Religion," "Mozart and the Jews," and—not least in my own affections —"Mozart's Dog." And since the story of Mozart does not really end with his death, some more recent aspects are examined under such titles as "Mozart's Cataloguers," "The Shavian Mozart," "How Mozart Became Mostly," and "Mozart at the Movies."

Perhaps from these chapters there may emerge a clearer picture of how Mozart saw the world of his time, and how the world of today sees him.

—Herbert Kupferberg

Key to Silhouettes

Silhouettes were a popular portrait form in the late eighteenth century. The name was derived from Étienne de Silhouette, a parsimonious financier who served as controller general of France in 1759. His hobby was cutting paper shadow portraits; the phrase *à la Silhouette* came to mean "on the cheap." All the persons depicted in the silhouettes used as chapter headings in this book were known to Mozart.

KEY TO SILHOUETTES

KEY TO SILHOUETTES

The First Mozart

"Next to God comes Papa."

—Mozart as a child.

iologically, psychologically, and musically, Wolfgang Amadeus Mozart would have been impossible without Leopold Mozart. The interaction of fathers and sons is one of the most imponderable and intriguing of human phenomena, and its complexities have rarely been demonstrated as vividly as in the case of the Mozarts. That sage Englishman, Dr. Samuel Johnson (whose dates, curiously, closely parallel those of Leopold Mozart), observed to James Boswell in 1763 that a struggle must always occur between father and son, for the former invariably seeks power and the latter independence.

Such a struggle began building in the Mozart family almost from the date of Wolfgang's birth, January 27, 1756, although it took more than two decades to flare into the open. Mozart's father taught him, guided him, encouraged him; he also dominated him, drove him, exploited him. Whether, on balance, he did more harm than good is a question that has been debated for two hundred years. The probability is that Leopold's control over his son's early life was musically beneficent but personally dubious. It was only after Mozart's wrenching break with his father in his early twenties that his true greatness flowered; until then it had been apparent only in flashes. As a man of everyday practicality and experience trying to channel and develop the course of genius, Leopold Mozart was to a certain extent a tragic figure. The relation between father and son, beset by tensions, anxieties, and disagreements, yet bonded by a profound love for each other, underlies the whole saga of Mozart and his music.

The Mozarts, unlike the Bachs, constituted no musical dynasty. The family came and went with almost startling suddenness. Leopold was a violinist who wrote a manual on how to play the instrument. Wolfgang, supreme as a composer and performer, produced little in the way of a musical progeny. Four of his six children died in infancy; of the two sons who survived, one became a minor diplomatic official, the other, talented pianistically, traded briefly on his father's repute, but left no lasting impression. Both sons died unmarried. Prior to Leopold and Wolfgang the name Mozart was unknown to history. Even their contemporaries had trouble spelling it. Among the forms in which it appears in various documents, records, journals, letters, and other writings of the time are Mozzart, Mozzard, Motzard, Motzart, Motzhart, Motzhard, Motzharth, Mozardt, Mozhardt, Mozhart, Moshart, Mozartz, Mozard, Muzard, Mazar and Mosar.

Leopold Mozart himself never became more than an orchestral player. His ambition was to be appointed director, or

Leopold Mozart at the age of fifty.

Kapellmeister, of the Salzburg court orchestra in which he was employed, but the highest rank he ever reached was that of vice Kapellmeister. In his early years as a musician, he tried his hand at composition, producing several dozen pieces, including symphonies and oratorios. A few still turn up as novelties at concerts from time to time. About thirty years ago musical scholars announced that the charming *Toy Symphony*, with parts for birdcalls, rattles, and tin horns, ascribed for generations to Joseph Haydn, was really the work of Leopold Mozart, being extracted from a work labeled "Cassatio ex G." Of such discoveries is musicology made.

Although he never achieved celebrity as a performer, Leopold made his name known as a pedagogue, through his textbook for violinists entitled *Versuch einer grundlichen Violinschule (Toward a Fundamental Violin Method)*, generally known as Leopold Mozart's *Violinschule*. Published in 1756, the year of Wolfgang's birth, it was translated into French, Dutch, and English, and still may be read in a modern edition. Aimed at the everyday player rather than the virtuoso, it affirmed, as few other books ever have, the dignity and importance of the orchestral musician:

> Decide now for yourself whether a good orchestral violinist is not of a far higher value than one who is purely a solo player. The latter can play everything according to his wishes, and arrange the style of the performance as he desires, or even for the convenience of his hand. But the former must possess the dexterity to understand and interpret the thoughts of different composers. . . . A solo player can, without great understanding of music, usually play his concertos fairly well—yea, even with distinction—but a good orchestral violinist must have deep insight into the whole art of musical composition.

Similarly, Leopold tried to inculcate respect for ordinary musicians in his son, who as he grew older developed an unfortunate tendency to display impatience—almost impertinence—toward musical minds that were slower than his own. When Wolfgang, aged twenty-four, was rehearsing his new opera *Idomeneo,* Leopold cautioned him to go out of his way to flatter and praise the players in the pit. "Every performer," he wrote him, "even the lowest viola player, is deeply moved by personal praise and becomes much more zealous and attentive, and a little courtesy of this kind will only cost you a word or two."

Delivering himself of homilies was part of Leopold Mozart's character. His letters and other recorded comments abound in Polonius-style advice and admonitions, often in Latin. Here are some of the maxims with which Leopold Mozart studded his correspondence and conversation:

> *"Aut Caesar aut nihil"* ("Either Caesar or nothing").
> *"Finis coronat opus"* ("Let the ending crown the work").
> *"Homo proponit, Deus disponit"* ("Man proposes, God disposes").
> "Nothing ventured, nothing won."
> "God will make everything right."
> "In Thee, God, I trust; Thy will be done."
> And, in a somewhat less pietistic mood:
> "It's all up to God, but we can help Him with some judicious planning and actions."

Wolfgang undoubtedly appreciated Leopold's advice, but he did not often act on it—sometimes, perhaps, to his own detriment. Leopold was fully aware of the extent of his son's genius and was increasingly disturbed by his apparent inability to make the most of it in a worldly sense. He once told Wolfgang that it was up to him whether he became "an ordinary musician, utterly forgotten by the world, or a famous Kapellmeister, of whom posterity will read."

To achieve the latter end, Leopold tried to force his son into his own mold. But as closely linked as the two were in their shared affection, respect, and musical intimacy, they were far apart in character and outlook. Leopold was a man of a dying generation and a fading political order. Wolfgang was no revolutionary—politics and social changes held little interest for him—but he lived in a revolutionary age and felt its effects. The semifeudal conventions and restrictions of his day were not for him, not because they were wrong in some abstract, theoretical way, but because he couldn't stand them personally. Franz Xaver Niemteschek, who knew him well and wrote one of the first biographies of him, said that Mozart could not bring himself to "bow and scrape" to obtain preferment.

Leopold on the other hand, though he was a cultivated and educated man, knew how to bow and scrape all too well. He had a family to support and a place in the community to maintain, in addition to a genius son to promote, and he prudently never challenged the courtly establishment that provided his income and security. The obsequiousness of his various "most humble and submissive" petitions to "His Serene Highness" the archbishop of Salzburg—often in an effort to advance the interests of his son—merely reflected the official formal language of the time, yet at times such subservience almost seemed to enter Leopold's very soul. He was frustrated by Wolfgang's repeated failures to make his way in the aristocratic world, even as he was heartened by each new evidence of his musical genius. To him there was both grief and joy in being the father of the greatest composer the world had seen.

Leopold Mozart was born in the Swabian city of Augsburg November 14, 1719, the son of a not very prosperous bookbinder. Modern tourists who take the "Romantic Road" from Munich northward are still shown his house as the bus rolls quickly by. Leopold, small and slight in stature but of handsome features, was an ambitious boy who was determined to move beyond his immediate surroundings. He attended the Jesuit seminary at Augsburg, studied theology and music, and at the age of seventeen decided to prepare for the priesthood at the University of Salzburg, a Benedictine institution. However two years there convinced him—and his superiors—that he was headed in the wrong direction; he was expelled for cutting classes too frequently. Deciding to make music his career, he took a job as fourth violinist in the orchestra of the local prince-archbishop.

Leopold spent the rest of his life (he lived to the age of sixty-seven) in Salzburg, working in the orchestra, composing, and giving lessons on the side. His pay was adequate if not munificent, and he became one of the solid citizens of the town. The two dwelling places in which he lived for nearly half-a-century, both still in existence, exude an air of bourgeois comfort.

At the age of twenty-eight Leopold married Anna Maria Pertl, a year younger than himself. She had been born in the village of St. Gilgen, not very far from Salzburg on the shores of the Wolfgangsee, or Lake Wolfgang. Her father, a county official and amateur musician, died when she was four, and her mother moved with her to Salzburg. When she met Leopold Mozart he was playing in the court orchestra, and after a rather prolonged courtship they were married in 1747. They were regarded, according to some contemporaries, as "the handsomest couple in Salzburg," and they lived together compatibly and affectionately. Leopold ran everybody's affairs, of course, but Anna Maria, motherly and gregarious, maintained a warm and tension-free household. On November 21, 1772, Leopold, then on a visit to Munich with Wolfgang, wrote to Anna Maria: "Today is the anniversary of our wedding day. It was twenty-five years ago, I think, that we had the sensible idea of getting married—an idea we had cherished, it is true, for many years. All good things take time!"

The Mozarts had seven children, but only two of them survived, their second, a girl they named Maria Anna but called Nannerl, and their seventh, a boy whose full baptismal name was Johannes Chrysostomus Wolfgangus Theophilus* Mozart —for short, Wolferl.

---

*Theophilus is the Greek form of the Latin Amadeus, which Mozart preferred, although he also answered to Amadé, Amadeo, and Gottlieb in French, Italian, and German. In all languages, the name means "beloved of God." One wonders whether he ever heard of the ancient Greek king Menander's saying: "Whom the gods love dies young."

The Prodigy Market

"God has let a miracle see the light in Salzburg. . . .
And if it ever is to become my duty to convince the
world of this miracle, the time is now, when people
ridicule and deny all miracles."

—Leopold Mozart, letter to Lorenz Hagenauer,
July 30, 1768

Child prodigies, musical and otherwise, were a matter of abiding fascination in the Europe into which Mozart was born. For years people had talked of the astounding feats of Christian Heinrich Heinecken, "The Wonder Child of Lübeck," born February 6, 1721. Christian Heinrich began to talk at the age of ten months, and, being of a religious turn of mind, was able to recount the principal incidents in the Pentateuch by the time he was two. He had learned French and Latin, in addition to his native German, at the age of three. The King of Denmark, hearing of his feats, invited him to visit his court and conversed briefly with him in Latin, after which the wunderkind, according to one eyewitness, recited a French verse "in honor of the princesses who were present." People from all over Germany flocked to Lübeck to hear the child discourse in three languages on religion and church history. Unfortunately Christian Heinrich died at the age of four, and so was never able to completely fulfill his promise.

Born the same year in Schwabach, near Nuremberg, was another youthful marvel, Jean-Philippe Baratier, the son of a Calvinist pastor whose family had emigrated from France after the revocation of the Edict of Nantes in 1685. Jean-Philippe also demonstrated precocity in infancy; he understood Greek, Latin, German, and French by age five, and shortly thereafter applied himself to Hebrew, Syriac, Chaldean, Arabic, and one or two other Eastern tongues.

At the age of twelve he completed his magnum opus, a translation from the original Hebrew into French of the narratives of Benjamin of Tudela, a Spanish Jew who traveled extensively through Europe and Asia Minor from 1165 to 1173. With its title page inscribed *Voyages de Rabbi Benjamin fils de Jona de Tudèle en Europe, en Asie et en Afrique depuis l'Espagne jusqu'à la Chine, Traduit de l'Hébreu,* Baratier's volume was published in Amsterdam in 1734.

About this time Jean-Philippe branched out into mathematics and devised a new method of calculating longitude at sea. He conveyed his system to the Academy of Sciences at Berlin, which promptly admitted him to membership. A few years later, while in Berlin, he was received by the King of Prussia, who—perhaps in jest—counseled him to take up the study of law since this was essential "to calling oneself a learned man." Baratier promptly spent the next fifteen months poring over law books and composing a comprehensive thesis upon the current state of public law. Understandably worn out, he was stricken with a fever and died October 5, 1740, in his nineteenth year.

Not surprisingly, Mozart's appearance as a six-year-old prodigy on the European scene prompted comparisons with both Heinecken and Baratier. On Wolfgang's first visit to Vienna in 1763, Count Thomas von Collalto, a nobleman at whose home he performed, was inspired to compose a poetic tribute to "The Little Six-Year-Old Clavier Player from Salzburg," concluding with the hope that young Mozart would, "not like Lübeck's child, too soon outwear" his welcome on this earth. During Mozart's childhood expedition to England, the Royal Society of London appointed a special commission of learned men to investigate the authenticity of his genius. Discussing prodigies of the past, their report noted that "amongst these, John Barratier (*sic*) hath been most particularly distinguished"; nevertheless, the conclusion was that Mozart was "most astonishing of all."

Mozart's remarkable talents first became evident when he was three years old. Leopold Mozart had already started his eldest child, Nannerl, on clavier lessons, and little Wolfgang used to sit himself down at the keyboard and imitate her with great delight. When he was four his father began to teach him as well as his sister; not only did he play various pieces correctly, but he began to produce little compositions of his own. His first piece is considered to be a minuet in G, which has been given the designation of Köchel No. 1.* At the age of four he attempted to write a clavier concerto; he also began playing the violin and at seven announced he wished to sit in on a quartet at home

*For Ludwig von Köchel and his system of cataloguing Mozart's works, see page 208.

Mozart at the age of six in court dress.

as second violinist. When his father said he didn't know enough, little Wolfgang indignantly replied: "You don't have to study to play second violin." Almost everything he did was done to music; when he carried his toys from one room to another he had those present sing or play a march. The only problem, his father said, was that it was difficult to teach him much because he already seemed to know everything by instinct. Once, when Wolfgang did make a small technical error in composing a trio, Leopold consoled himself with the thought that this would at least prove that the child had written it himself.

Although other musical prodigies existed in Mozart's time, none made the same kind of extraordinary impact. A child violinist named Gertrud Elisabeth Schmeling, born seven years before Wolfgang, excited audiences in Vienna and London with her prowess, especially when her peculiar history became known. Her mother had died shortly after her birth and her father, who earned a poor living as a musical instrument repairman, carried her around with him when he went out on a job. To prevent her wandering off he would tie her to a chair, a practice that apparently led to her developing a bad case of rickets. At the age of four, Gertrud picked up a fiddle and, without benefit of instruction, not only drew sounds from it but began playing scales. Her delighted father quickly gave her lessons and put her on exhibition in his native town of Kassel in Germany, where she soon was earning more money than he was. Her health improved and she began to tour more widely. A British diplomat who heard her in Vienna urged Schmeling to take her to England, where she played at court at age eleven.

In England, however, several of her patrons advised her that the violin was not a ladylike instrument, and since she had a bright soprano voice, suggested she take up singing instead. This she did, studying with the Italian pedagogue Pietro Domenico

Paradies, who had settled in London. Paradies taught her to sing; however, he also apparently gave her other, more intimate instruction which persuaded her father to break off the lessons.

Back on the Continent, Gertrud launched a highly successful career as a singer, becoming a favorite at the court of Frederick the Great and a specialist in Handel's bravura operas. She married a cellist named Giovanni Battista Mara, and it was under the name of Gertrud Mara that she became the first German soprano to achieve international eminence.

Mozart never met Mara in her violin-prodigy days, but he did encounter her as a singer and was not overly impressed either with her personality or her voice. He heard her in Munich while he was there working on his opera *Idomeneo* and reported that she was lacking in art and had "conceit, arrogance and unblushing *effronterie*" written on her face.

Mozart's own success as a child prodigy seemed to open the floodgates, and an outpouring of would-be emulators appeared on the scene. One was a Viennese child named François-Joseph Darcis, who surfaced in France at age twelve only to be dismissed as "a little abortion" by one observer who pronounced him vastly inferior to "the young and charming Mozart." Another, William Crotch, began playing the organ at two-and-a-half and gave concerts in London at four. But despite being widely advertised as "the English Mozart" he never really displayed any creative talent and wound up as a professor of music and was appointed in 1822 as principal of the Royal Academy of Music.

Mozart himself appears to have looked skeptically at the crop of child prodigies who were almost glutting the market. In 1777, when he was twenty-one, he wrote his father a derisive account of the playing of Nanette Stein, the eight-year-old daughter of Johann Andreas Stein, the most famous keyboard-instrument maker of the day. Punning on the family name he observed:

"Anyone who sees and hears her play and can keep from laughing must, like her father, be made of stone (*Stein*)." He went on to describe in detail the little girl's facial grimaces, awkward posture, and failure to keep time, the latter being, he remarked, "the most difficult and the prime requisite in music."

Mozart's childhood violin, now at the Mozart Museum in Salzburg.

However, he conceded that Miss Stein had innate talent, and he promised her father to help develop it. Mozart, like many great musicians, hated teaching, but he was always ready to assist a promising and willing young performer. In 1786 a boy of eight named Johann Nepomuk Hummel was brought to Mozart, then thirty, by his father with the hope that he might be given a few lessons. Mozart was reluctant but finally agreed to hear the boy play. "Sit down at the piano and show us what you can do," he said.

Hummel—who eventually was to become a celebrated pianist and composer himself—played piece after piece while Mozart listened with growing interest. Finally he turned to the father and said, "I'll teach him, but I want him to live with me so I can keep an eye on him. I'll give him free lessons, lodging, and food. Something can be made of him."

Though his own financial condition was none too strong at the time, Mozart kept Hummel in his home for two years, sponsored his debut at a concert in Dresden, introduced him to the leading musical figures of the day, and saw his career on its way. Thus did one true prodigy respond to another.

On the Road

"People who do not travel—that is, those who are interested in the arts and learning—are miserable folk indeed."

—Mozart, letter to his father,
September 11, 1778

olfgang Amadeus Mozart was a traveling man. He began touring Europe when he was six years old, accompanied by his father, mother, and sister; undertook many other trips during his childhood and adolescence; and even when he settled permanently in Vienna in 1781 was always ready to take to the road whenever he thought he would profit thereby either artistically or financially.

Such mobility hardly seems noteworthy nowadays, when musicians jet around the world with casual frequency. But traveling any distance in Mozart's time was not only tedious and time-consuming, it also was grueling and dangerous. Leopold Mozart was nonetheless determined to take Wolfgang and his sister on the road. Salzburg was a comfortable town and Leopold's employer, the archbishop who ruled the city, maintained a decent musical establishment. But if Wolfgang's talents were to gain adequate recognition they would have to be displayed in such great centers of musical activity as Vienna, Munich, Mannheim, Paris, and London, difficult as it might be to reach those distant cities.

Leopold has been accused of seeking to exploit his children's talents out of crassness, but there is not the slightest indication of anything besides love, tenderness, and mutual concern within the family during those early years. Both Mozart children loved what they were doing and seem to have emerged as reasonably well-adjusted human beings from their unusual childhoods. Undoubtedly Leopold hoped to make money from his children's musical exhibitions. He kept careful accounts of receipts and expenses during the family tours, and complained bitterly when payments were less than anticipated. But wealth was not his major motivation. He several times expressed pride that the traveling entourage always managed to cover its expenses; beyond that one senses that he might have been satisfied had his son ever managed to obtain a permanent musical position that would bring him prestige, security, and a good, steady income.

Leopold Mozart served the family not only as a husband and parent, but as major domo, impresario, treasurer, and travel agent. Whether or not he was going along, he made all the arrangements, selected the itineraries, reserved the accommodations, prepared letters of credit, and provided appropriately phrased written introductions to officials and dignitaries in cities along the way.

Railroads didn't come to Austria until 1823, so in Mozart's time all travelers still had to cope with the exigencies and frustrations of eighteenth-century stagecoach transport. Conditions were execrable, with muddy and bumpy roads, comfortless vehicles, and frequent delays caused either by the need to change horses or to meet the border formalities of each small principality. Accidents were frequent; driving the team of four horses that hauled a typical stagecoach was so difficult that the art gave rise to the English words *coach* and *coaching* in the sense of "teacher" or "teaching." It took five days to get from Florence to Rome, less than 200 miles. To cover seven miles an hour was considered making good time.

Passengers, usually six to a coach, rode all day, often arising before dawn to get started; they spent the nights at inns along the way, usually uncomfortably. Discomfort often gave way to danger; on one trip a wheel of the Mozarts' conveyance broke, so that Leopold and another passenger had to get out and walk to lighten the load until they could reach the next town for repairs. On a voyage to Italy, Leopold suffered a badly injured leg when a two-wheeled carriage collapsed in the road.

Basically there were three ways of traveling. One could go by the mail coach, which carried passengers in addition to postal material; one could engage a place on the commercial stagecoaches that plied between cities; or one could buy or hire a private vehicle, which meant paying for the driver and for the relays of fresh horses along the way.

Leopold chose this last and most expensive method for his grand tour in 1763. In the first place, he was out to conquer Europe, which meant impressing the aristocracy; in the second, he was traveling with his wife and two young children who, he considered, deserved as much comfort as he could provide. He also took along a servant named Sebastian Winter, who left him in Paris to take a better job, and a portable clavier purchased from Andreas Stein. The Mozarts traveled in style.

They also were received in style. Public concertgoing as we know it today was barely coming into existence; the accepted way to gain musical celebrity, not to mention financial reward, was to appear at court or in the salons of the nobility.

That was the course followed by Leopold with Wolfgang and his sister. It's difficult to say whether the aristocrats for whom the children performed were really interested in their musical skills or whether they regarded them as traveling freaks, passing sensations like the legendary wunderkind of Lübeck. Maria Theresa, the strong-willed and rather sour Holy Roman Empress, who ruled Austria for forty years, praised Wolfgang so warmly when he played for her at Schönbrunn Palace that the delighted child jumped into her lap and kissed her. But ten years later, when one of her sons, the archduke of Milan, suggested giving Mozart, then sixteen, a permanent post, she replied frostily that she didn't approve of people who "go about the world like beggars." Obviously Mozart didn't grow on her with age.

Little Wolfgang also played for royalty in Paris. This time the court was that of Louis XV, and again everyone marveled at him, although—according to one of the innumerable clever-child stories that spread about him—he is alleged to have complained bitterly when Madame de Pompadour, unlike Maria Theresa, declined to kiss him.

The last, and longest, stop on the Mozarts' tour was London, where the Mozarts had hopes of making considerable money. Leopold, in a letter to his Salzburg friend, landlord and banker, Lorenz Hagenauer, reported that the entire family had made "a heavy deposit in vomiting" during the crossing of the English Channel, with himself setting the pace. He had engaged a private boat to carry his party of six (himself, his wife, his two children, and two servants) and, since there was extra room aboard, he rented out places to four other travelers. The cost of the crossing to him, he estimated, was 3 guineas, or about $75.*

Perhaps with the memory of the Channel crossing still vivid, the Mozarts remained in England from April 1764, to July 1765, well over a year. (Their return trip from Dover to Calais, as it turned out, took only three and a half hours and was made on a smooth sea "with a healthy stomach.") The reigning monarch in England was George III and he, like his counterparts in Vienna and Paris, received the Mozarts with friendliness if no great monetary recompense. The king, along with Queen Charlotte and other onlookers, put Wolfgang through his usual paces. He was asked to play difficult pieces at sight, accompany the queen in an aria, compose variations, and do the trick of playing on a keyboard covered with a cloth. Wolfgang even composed a brief chorus to the words "God is our refuge and strength, a very present help in trouble" (K. 20). This anthem was his first effort in choral writing and the only text he ever set in English. Leopold presented the manuscript to the British Museum, which acknowledged it in a cordial letter.

Most musicians seem to have taken Wolfgang perfectly seriously, treating the eight-year-old boy as an equal, discussing technical matters with him, and listening to him attentively both in performance and conversation. Among the prominent figures he met was Johann Christian Bach, illustrious son of the great Johann Sebastian. Johann Christian, having settled in England, played a leading role in London's musical life. He welcomed the German-speaking child warmly. On one occasion, Bach took Wolfgang between his knees as he sat at an organ console and

*See "A Note on Currency Values," page 256.

Wolfgang's anthem "God is our refuge."

he and the boy took turns playing the instrument. Onlookers said it was impossible to tell where the one left off and the other began. Christian Bach, who wrote in the contemporary, smoothly classical "gallant" style, quite unlike his father's rugged polyphony, exercised considerable influence upon the composing style of the susceptible young boy.

England was well ahead of most Continental cities in giving public concerts, as distinguished from specially arranged private performances for the aristocracy. They had been first instituted, around 1672, by one John Banister, and were now presented at several locations. After attending a number of public concerts in London, Leopold decided to have Wolfgang give one of his own. To his surprise and pleasure, an audience of several hundred,

Johann Christian Bach, who befriended Wolfgang in England.

"including all the leading people in London," turned out for it, and most of the members of the orchestra refused to accept any payment for accompanying such a gifted child.

Leopold quickly arranged for additional concerts at convenient gathering places, including taverns, and advertised them with almost hucksterish enthusiasm. This is a typical notice from the *Public Advertizer* for June, 1765:

To all Lovers of Sciences.

The greatest Prodigy that Europe, or that even Human Nature has to boast of, is, without Contradiction, the little German Boy WOLFGANG MOZART; a Boy, Eight Years Old*, who has, and indeed very justly, raised the Admiration not only of the greatest Men, but also of the greatest Musicians in Europe. It is hard to say, whether his Execution upon the Harpsichord and his playing and singing at sight, or his own Caprice, Fancy, and Compositions for all Instruments, are most astonishing. The Father of this Miracle, being obliged by Desire of several Ladies and Gentlemen to postpone, for a very short time, his Departure from England, will give an Opportunity to hear this little Composer and his Sister, whose musical knowledge wants not Apology. Performs every Day in the Week, from Twelve to Three o'Clock in the Great Room, at the Swan and Hoop, Cornhill. Admittance 2s. 6d. each Person. The two Children will play also together with four hands upon the same Harpsichord, and put upon it a Handkerchief, without seeing the Keys.

The Mozarts' stay in England was not without problems; besides several illnesses that laid the children up for short periods, Leopold himself was stricken for a time, necessitating a cancellation of all activities. The English, he reported to Hagenauer, have "a kind of native complaint which they call a *cold*"; Leopold himself caught such a bad one that he had to be "clystered, purged and bled" and, finally, spend seven weeks

*Wolfgang was actually nine.

resting and recuperating outside of London at Chelsea, where the climate was said to be more salubrious.

In addition, some of the novelty of Wolfgang's feats inevitably began to wear off, and concert audiences diminished. Even a reduction of prices and newspaper advertisements urging people to see "the prodigies of nature" failed to bring in the former crowds, and Leopold decided it was time to lead his little musical troupe back to Salzburg. It took them nearly six months to get there, for they traveled at a leisurely pace through Holland, Switzerland, France, and Germany, stopping whenever they visited a fair-sized city to give a concert or to visit the local court.

Thus Wolfgang Mozart spent three and a half years, from the ages of six to ten, as a traveling prodigy. Never during that time, nor, for that matter, at any other time during his life, did he set foot inside a schoolroom. His formal instruction, nonmusical as well as musical, came from his father. Wolfgang especially loved arithmetic; he was said to cover not only sheets of paper but tablecloths and wallpaper with rows of figures. On a subsequent visit to Italy he begged his sister to mail him copies of a series of mathematical tables he had lost. Geography he certainly had every opportunity to apprehend at first hand, and languages he seemed to pick up readily. He spoke Italian well enough that a cardinal he encountered at the Vatican at the age of thirteen complimented him on his fluency. He spoke adequate French and wrote several letters in that language; he also knew a little English and in later life took lessons from some British friends in Vienna.

Despite all this absorption of knowledge, Wolfgang was not an educated man in the sense that his father was. Nor did he enjoy anything like a normal childhood, for, aside from his sister, he was denied the regular companionship of other children. Instead he spent his formative years among pompous royal personages, curious or skeptical aristocrats, and mature but not necessarily enlightened musicians. It was an environment that might have bored, stifled, or irritated most children, but it appears to have not had the least such depressing effect upon Mozart. In fact, he loved every minute of it.

Writing to Hagenauer from London, Leopold Mozart said of "our invincible Wolfgang," now aged eight: "What he knew when we left Salzburg is but a shadow compared to what he knows now." The only thing Leopold overlooked was that his growing son, having once seen London, Paris, and Vienna, would never again be content to stay in Salzburg.

Nannerl

"Nannerl no longer suffers by comparison with the boy, for she plays so beautifully that everyone talks about her and admires her technique."

—Leopold Mozart, letter to Lorenz Hagenauer, August 20, 1763

It is a curious coincidence that the two most notable musical child prodigies who ever lived, Wolfgang Mozart and Felix Mendelssohn, each had a sister four years older than himself who was an accomplished pianist and composer. Had Maria Anna Mozart, born in 1751, and Fanny Mendelssohn, born in 1805, lived in later eras they might well have had fruitful musical careers of their own. The Mendelssohn family considered it unladylike for a young woman to perform in public or to publish her music; the Mozarts had fewer inhibitions, but once

Wolfgang's unique genius manifested itself poor Maria Anna—
or Nannerl, as she was invariably known—was shunted aside
brusquely.

And yet at the beginning Nannerl was the apple of her
father's eye. He started her at the clavier at the age of six and
was delighted to find her responsive to music. In fact, he prepared for her a collection of practice pieces, some by himself,
some by other composers, which he called "The Nannerl Notebook." It was while listening to his sister at her keyboard practice
that Wolfgang began to display his own musical interest by
climbing up onto the bench and playing chords.

Between her own innate musicality and skill, and Leopold's
expert instruction, Nannerl became a superb young performer.
Leopold noted that she played the most difficult compositions
with precision; during the family's grand tour of Europe Nannerl
was adjudged Wolfgang's equal in pianistic brilliance, being excelled by him only in improvisation and composing variations.
In 1764 Leopold Mozart, whose pride in his children never
degenerated into mere boasting, wrote: "My little girl, though
she is only twelve years old, is one of the most skillful clavier
players in Europe." Wolfgang, when he was all of fourteen,
complimented her on some of her compositions. "I am amazed
to find how well you can compose," he wrote her. "In a word
the song is beautiful." Unfortunately, none of Nannerl Mozart's
compositions has survived.

Nannerl went along with her brother on four child-prodigy
tours, including of course the great three-year expedition through
the Continent and England. At the urging of Leopold she even
kept a kind of travel diary in which she utilized the language
of each country the family visited, so that one can still read, in
English, her notes of their excursions to London Bridge and a
foundling hospital.

But in 1769 Leopold set off with Wolfgang on a fifth trip, this time to Italy, leaving both his daughter—now fifteen— and his wife at home. Nannerl may not have realized it at the time, but this was the effective end of her career as a public performer, for henceforth Leopold devoted his promotional endeavors strictly to his son. Nannerl managed only a few journeys out of Salzburg, to Munich in 1775 to attend the premiere of Wolfgang's opera *La finta giardiniera*, and to the same city in 1781 for his *Idomeneo*.

For the most part, Nannerl remained at home with her parents and, after the death of her mother, with her father alone. She ran the household, gave occasional piano lessons, and conducted a lively correspondence with her brother, retailing all the town news and gossip. They had shared an unusual childhood, visited many strange places together, and developed close bonds. Warmth, affection, and playfulness pervade their correspondence. Wolfgang teased her about her Salzburg boyfriends, sent her doggerel, indulged in his penchant for bawdy humor.

And yet they inevitably grew apart, particularly after Wolfgang settled permanently in Vienna and married. Neither Nannerl nor Leopold Mozart approved Wolfgang's choice of a wife, and a hostility developed between the sister and the sister-in-law, which persisted even in their old age when chance brought them both back to live as neighbors in Salzburg.

Unlike Wolfgang, whose stature was slight and appearance unprepossessing, Nannerl grew into a tall and beautiful young woman. In her late teens one observer described her as having "ripened into a graceful girl with long auburn hair, blue eyes and well-turned shoulders" and added that she "delighted every assembly not less by her beauty than by her talent."

Although Nannerl had been courted for a number of years

Nannerl Mozart at the age of eleven in court dress.

by some of Salzburg's most eligible bachelors, she did not marry until 1784, when she was thirty-two. Wolfgang had married two years previously. Nannerl's husband was a native Salzburger who had become a magistrate of the town of St. Gilgen, her mother's birthplace, a half-day's coach trip away. His name was Johann Baptist von Sonnenburg, he was forty-seven years old, and twice a widower with five children. Nannerl herself had three children by him, so she presided over a busy household.

After her marriage, Nannerl and her father exchanged letters almost daily, much of their correspondence revolving around Wolfgang and his problems and achievements in Vienna. Wolfgang for the most part continued writing only sporadically to his sister; while his notes were affectionate, they also were brief, accompanied by an explanation that he was too busy to write more. Their correspondence grew rather more formal when Leopold died in 1787 and his estate was at issue. Wolfgang, after rather stiffly pointing out that he had to guard the interests of his own wife and child, finally agreed to let Nannerl buy out his share of the legacy for a flat payment of 1,000 gulden, about $5,000.

In 1801 Nannerl's husband died and she returned to Salzburg with her children and stepchildren. She far outlived her brother, dying in 1829 at the age of seventy-eight. In Salzburg she supported herself by giving piano lessons; it was said her pupils could always be identified by their light touch and graceful style. As she grew older she became increasingly afflicted by illness and poverty. Shortly before her death she received a visit from Vincent and Mary Novello, of the British music publishing family, who came to present her with a gift of money raised by English admirers of her brother's music. They found her totally blind, nearly deaf, leading a frugal and lonely existence. The Novellos were there not only to do an act of charity but to gather as much information as they could about Wolfgang, whose music had become popular in England. Mozart's second son, Franz Xaver, there on a visit, served as interpreter. Nannerl answered as best she could, in a way reliving the exciting days of her youth. Indeed, there were many who came to her after Mozart's death to write down what she could tell them about the great musician whose childhood she had shared. She ended her life as she began it, sharing, at least in a small way, the glory of her illustrious younger brother.

Mozart in Italy

"Wolfgang in Germany, Amadeo in Italy."

—signature of a letter from Mozart to his sister,
February 10, 1770

eopold Mozart planned his son's conquest of Europe with almost military precision and thoroughness. By the time Wolfgang was twelve years old he had been paraded through England, France, Switzerland, and the Low Countries in addition to such Hapsburg cities as Vienna, Munich, and even Brno in Moravia.

Now it was time for him to go to Italy. He was passing from the child prodigy stage to the young composer stage. Incredible as it seems to us (and, for that matter, as it seemed to many of his contemporaries), he had already written half a dozen symphonies, three piano concertos, two operas, *La finta semplice* and *Bastien and Bastienne*, and a variety of other works.

33

Leopold knew that Italy was the musical heartland of Europe. Most of the composers in Vienna, for example, were Italians, as were many of the performers, particularly the singers. In fact, even a musical backwater like Salzburg had several Italian performers attached to its court, among them a violinist named Brunetti and a castrato singer named Ceccarelli.

Salzburg was not far from the Italian frontier, but it was no mere border crossing that Leopold had in mind. From December 1769, to March 1771, a period of well over a year, Wolfgang, who was thirteen, traveled with his father almost the length of the Italian peninsula, crisscrossing from city to city. For Leopold, who had obtained a leave of absence from his employer, the prince-archbishop of Salzburg, it was an effort to establish his son as a young genius-composer; for Wolfgang it was an opportunity to meet some of the leading musical performers and creators of the day. A brief listing of some of the stops and some of the encounters may give an idea of the musical, and other, adventures that befell the travelers.

Verona This was their first major stop after entering Italy by way of the Brenner Pass. Here Wolfgang was invited to give several concerts before an audience of notables, and to play the organ at the Church of St. Tommaso. An artist named Saverio dalla Rosa painted his portrait; local poets incribed verses in his honor; the bishop of Verona and other dignitaries invited him to lunch. The Mozarts also did some sightseeing, visiting the famous Arena which, more than a century later, was to become the site of a summer opera festival.

Mantua Here everybody of importance in town wished to hear Wolfgang demonstrate his skills as a performer and improviser. He also gave a free concert at which he directed the Philharmonic Academy of Mantua in several of his own works.

A local newspaper pronounced him "a miracle in music" and he was courteously received by Niccolò Piccinni, the famous Italian rival of Gluck. Wolfgang fired off letters written to his sister in Italian, and ventured into operatic criticism. After seeing Johann Adolf Hasse's opera *Demetrio* he reported: "The prima donna sings well but softly . . . the seconda donna resembles a grenadier and has a powerful voice. . . . Prima ballerina—good. They say she is no dog but I have not seen her up close."

Milan Once again, a warm reception from the local nobility. Wolfgang met Giovanni Battista Sammartini, one of the city's most venerable and honored composers. Perhaps the most important event was that the governor general of Lombardy commissioned an opera (*Mitridate, rè di Ponto*) from him for the following Christmas, a considerable distinction to confer upon a fourteen-year-old boy (he had just marked his birthday). However, it was at Milan that Leopold began to realize that the Italians, like the French, were more ready to pay in compliments than in cash, and that he very likely would be taking little money home with him from the tour.

Lodi Here at an inn on March 15, 1770, Wolfgang composed his first string quartet, in G Major (K. 80).

Parma Wolfgang and his father were both fascinated by their first encounter with a singer named Lucrezia Agujari, the natural child of an Italian nobleman. She made a professional asset of her illegitimate birth by billing herself as La Bastardella or La Bastardina. Her vocal range was stupendous; Wolfgang noted in a letter that her "gallant gullet" could produce a C *in altissimo* and reach down three octaves below that.

Florence Wolfgang had the usual round of successes while Leopold for once gave way to some touristic enthusiasm, writing to his wife: "I should like you to see Florence and the sur-rounding countryside; you would say that one ought to live and die here."

Florence also was the scene of one of the more touching personal incidents of Wolfgang's younger days: his brief friend-ship with Thomas Linley, a musical prodigy of his own age. Linley was an English boy who, as a gifted violinist, had been sent to study in Italy with Pietro Nardini, one of the great masters of the instrument. The two boys were introduced by a poetess, Maddalena Morelli, and a warm friendship sprang up between them. They played violin duets together and gave a joint concert. When they had to separate—the Mozarts re-mained in Florence only ten days—both boys wept, and To-massino, as Wolfgang called his friend, presented him with a valedictory sonnet he had written. Wolfgang corresponded with Thomas for a while, and in later years always asked after him whenever he met a traveling English musician. Unfortunately, Linley's life proved even briefer than Mozart's; he drowned at age twenty-one while swimming in a pond near London.

Rome The Mozarts remained there for two weeks, during which Wolfgang achieved one of his most celebrated feats, which, in a later age, might have become known as the Great Allegri Caper.

Gregorio Allegri had been an Italian contrapuntal composer, a follower of the great Giovanni da Palestrina. Allegri lived in Rome from 1582 to 1652 and wrote much church choral music, but his chief claim to fame is that he composed a *Miserere* of such distinction that it was performed only at the Sistine Chapel of the Vatican and nowhere else.

It is not at all clear why church officials guarded Allegri's *Miserere* so closely. It was a complex piece for two choirs, between them singing nine parts, with a text taken from the Book of Psalms. First given in the reign of Pope Urban VIII around 1630, it was performed every year by the Papal Choir during Holy Week and its publication was prohibited upon pain of excommunication. No one was permitted to copy it out; even the singers who performed the work had to turn in the sheets from which they worked after each rehearsal. The only possible reason for these strict prohibitions may have been the piece's vocal ornamentation, which were considered unusually difficult and beautiful.

Actually three copies of the *Miserere* had been made available by various Popes to such recipients as Emperor Leopold I, the king of Portugal, and Padre Martini of Bologna, the great musical theoretician and pedagogue. How seriously people took the threat of excommunication by Mozart's day is questionable; just the same, nobody dared to copy down the music.

Mozart and his father arrived in Rome during Holy Week of 1770 and naturally they went to hear the *Miserere*. Wolfgang listened closely, returned to their quarters, took pen and ink, and wrote the whole piece down from memory. Leopold wrote triumphantly to his wife: "We have it! . . . We shall bring it home with us!!"

Wolfgang's feat indeed became the talk of cultivated people everywhere, almost passing into musical folklore. There were those who took heart from his personal daring as well as being impressed by his musical acumen. Some fifteen years after his death Marie Walewska, the beautiful Polish patriot who became Napoleon's mistress and the mother of his illegitimate son Alexandre, heard another performance of Allegri's *Miserere* in the Sistine Chapel and was so moved that she wrote to a friend: "Do you know that until recently the work could be heard only in St. Peter's and the Vatican? There was some order against

CAV. AMADEO WOLFGANGO MOZART ACCAD. FILARMON: DI BOLOG. E DI VERONA

The "completely lifelike" portrait of Mozart wearing the Order of the Golden Spur.

transcribing it, under pain of excommunication. But Mozart was not afraid. He transcribed it; and others followed suit. So it is thanks to him that you may hear it now in Warsaw or Vienna."

Evidently Pope Clement XIV didn't take Mozart's transgression too seriously, for he subsequently conferred upon the boy the Order of the Golden Spur, a distinction that entitled the holder to be known as "Cavaliere" or "Chevalier" the rest of his life. Unlike the distinguished but somewhat stuffy Christoph Willibald Gluck, who always insisted on being called "the Chevalier Gluck," Wolfgang never bothered with the title although, probably at the insistence of Leopold, he had a portrait painted in 1777 showing him wearing the decoration of the Order.

Curiously, Allegri's *Miserere* is pretty much of a dead letter nowadays. When was the last time anybody heard it in America?

Naples   The Mozarts spent over a month in Naples, the southernmost point of their journeys. Sightseeing and music-making—not necessarily in that order—made up their agenda. Wolfgang watched Vesuvius smoke ("thunder and lightning and all the rest," he reported to Nannerl), visited Pompeii and Herculaneum, took a boat ride on the Mediterranean, and bought copper engravings of all the sights to show his mother and sister. He also met celebrated musicians like Niccolo Jommelli and Giovanni Paisiello, attended a number of performances, and gave several of his own. Among those who received the Mozarts cordially was the British Ambassador, William Hamilton. His wife Catherine was a fine pianist, but Leopold reported amusedly that "she trembled at having to play before Wolfgang." Incidentally, after Catherine's death in 1782 Lord Hamilton took a second Lady Hamilton, Emma, who was to become the notorious mistress of Admiral Nelson.

Bologna   Naples, which they left in June, marked the midpoint in time of the Mozarts' Italian journey. They spent the next eight months on a leisurely trip back north, revisiting many of the places in which they had stopped on their southward trip. Among these were Rome and Milan—where Mozart's opera *Mitridate* was presented to great acclaim. They also visited

Venice, Turin, and other towns they had missed on the way down.

The most significant of their northward stopovers was Bologna, where they stayed three months. The purpose of this prolonged visit was to permit Wolfgang to study with Giovanni Battista Martini, the illustrious Padre Martini, a Franciscan priest who was probably the greatest musical teacher of his day. Martini, one of the few musicians with enough insight to realize the extent of Mozart's incipient genius, took him under his wing and established an affectionate relationship that persisted between the old man and the young for a number of years.

Wolfgang was also installed as a member of the Philharmonic Academy of Bologna, a musical society with stringent admission requirements and a minimum age of twenty. Wolfgang was six years younger, but after examining him the members of the academy voted unanimously to waive the age requirement. A similar honor was accorded him by the Academy of Verona.

Mozart and his father finally returned to Salzburg in March 1771, but three months afterward they went again to Milan, where Wolfgang's "dramatic serenade" *Ascanio in Alba*, a work celebrating the marriage of one of Maria Theresa's sons, Archduke Ferdinand, was staged. Later there was another six-month trip to Milan during which another opera, *Lucio Silla*, was performed.

Needless to say, Wolfgang enjoyed these trips and reveled in the Italian climate, the musical no less than the meteorological. "I have never had so much honor and appreciation anywhere as I had in Italy," he wrote home. Leopold, on the other hand, seems to have developed a certain uneasiness; the voyages to Italy did not show a net fiscal profit, and while Wolfgang received several important commissions, they neither set a continuing

Wolfgang and his father combined to write this letter home
from Milan on December 18, 1772, while he was completing his
opera *Lucio Silla*. The sketch in the center conveys Wolfgang's
greetings to his sister.

pattern nor seemed likely to lead to a permanent post. One
observer, the veteran composer Hasse, observed shrewdly that
while Wolfgang was possessed of much "natural good sense,"
Leopold Mozart "as far as I can see, is equally discontented
everywhere. . . . He idolizes his son a little too much." One is
left with the impression that when Leopold returned to Salzburg

it was with the feeling that the Italians, despite all their pro-testations, did not really appreciate Mozart's music.

Leopold's forebodings have been substantiated by the course of Mozart's music in Italy since his death. Italian audiences, particularly operatic audiences, tend to listen to his works with politeness rather than enthusiasm. This has been true since the start. The first production of *Don Giovanni* in Rome in 1811, though carefully prepared, achieved respectful praise but no demand for a repetition. At its Milan premiere three years later actual hissing was heard. Most listeners regarded the music as antiquated and "learned" rather than in the popular vein they preferred.

A good deal of this attitude persists. Edward J. Dent, the British musical scholar, observed in the early twentieth century that "the Italian public obviously and naturally prefers Rossini." Giuseppe Verdi, the greatest of Italian operatic composers, ex-pressed a deep respect for Bach, but he dismissed Mozart as a *quartettista*—a writer of string quartets. A number of Italian singers, such as the bass Ezio Pinza and the tenor Tito Schipa, became superb Mozart performers, but his music has never been an Italian operatic specialty. Even the greatest of Italian con-ductors, Arturo Toscanini, rarely conducted Mozart's operas, his major effort in this direction being *The Magic Flute*, which he directed both at La Scala and at the Salzburg Festival of 1937. In 1956, Italy was one of the few European countries to hold no official celebration of the 200th anniversary of Mozart's birth, with its observation left strictly up to local opera com-panies and orchestras.

Although he little suspected it at the time, Mozart's suc-cessful youthful forays into Italy represented a personal rather than a musical triumph. And once his years of adolescence were over, he never went back.

Mozart's Dog

"Bimperl, I trust, is doing her duty and cuddling up to you, for she is a good and faithful fox-terrier."

—Anna Maria Mozart,
letter to Leopold Mozart,
October 2, 1777

It may seem excessive to devote an entire chapter of a book about Mozart to his dog, but pets have a way of playing revealing roles in human lives. As fiction's most discerning detective, Mr. Sherlock Holmes, sagely observed in that curious story "The Adventure of the Creeping Man": "A dog reflects the family life. Whoever saw a frisky dog in a gloomy family, or a sad dog in a happy one?"

Mozart's dog, a small female fox terrier, was named Bimperl, and, judging by the family correspondence, occupied a good portion of his time and thought. Bimperl appeared on the scene in 1773, when Mozart was seventeen, presumably as a puppy, for she was still around some ten years later. She is mentioned for the first time in a letter of Wolfgang's that same year, written from Vienna to his sister. It was a typically breezy Mozart letter, with his name signed backward as Gnagflow Trazom—a custom he playfully adopted from time to time. "How is Miss Bimbes?—please give her all sorts of messages from me," he wrote. Miss Bimbes was the dog's formal name, but like the rest of the family she was known by a diminutive. For years Mozart continued to send his regards to the dog from cities all over Europe. Describing the triumph of his youthful opera *La finta giardiniera* in Munich to his mother in January of 1775 he wound up his report: "Adieu. 1000 smacks to Bimperl."

While Bimperl's cognitive powers may not have matched those of Ulysses' dog Argos, who recognized his master instantly when he returned after being away twenty years at the Trojan War, she nevertheless appears to have been a reasonably clever dog. Her particular delight was Spanish snuff. Leopold Mozart reported admiringly that she would select the box containing Spanish snuff from four or five others on a table and scratch on it until someone gave her a pinch to lick up. Mozart's mother was particularly solicitous of the dog; when she was away traveling she would write to Nannerl with strict instructions as to her care and feeding. Altogether there were over twenty references to Bimperl in the family correspondence.

One of the lowest ebbs in Bimperl's life, as indeed that of the entire Mozart clan, came in September of 1777, when Wolfgang, at the age of twenty-one, set out, with his mother as a traveling companion, for a prolonged journey that was to end in tragedy in Paris. Leopold, who was sending his wife and son off with misgivings, reported that the entire household, including

A silhouette, by an eighteenth-century French designer, said to be of the Mozart family.

the dog, had spent a doleful day following the departure of the two travelers. Nannerl lay down with a headache in a darkened room, and Bimperl crawled in beside her. Leopold also took to his bed, only to be awakened when the whimpering dog asked to be taken out for a walk.

Later on Nannerl wrote to her brother with the hearty expressiveness that characterizes so much of the family correspondence: "Miss Bimpes too lives on in hope, for she stands or sits near the door for half-hours on end, thinking that every minute you are going to return. All the same, she is quite well, eats, drinks, sleeps, shits and pisses." Weeks later Bimperl was still waiting anxiously. Leopold reported that whenever he and Nannerl left the house for a time the dog would think that "because she has lost you two, she is now going to lose us as well," and would almost "choke with joy" with her yelpings when they returned.

Wolfgang's last recorded reference to Bimperl occurred in 1782, shortly before his marriage in Vienna. "A pinch of Spanish snuff for Bimperl!" he said in a letter to his father. Presumably Bimperl, who had attained a respectable old age, died soon after.

During his ten years of residence in Vienna, Mozart appears to have acquired at least two other dogs, named respectively Goukerl and Katherl, unless indeed these are two different names for one and the same animal—a question which might possibly engage the attention of scholars seeking new areas of Mozartean research.

Dogs were by no means the only pets that Mozart acquired during his lifetime. As a child in London he once abruptly broke off a demonstration at the harpsichord, rushing from the instrument to run after a pet cat which had just wandered into the room. At various times the Mozart household in Salzburg boasted a pet grasshopper and several canaries. Mozart owned a songbird at the time of his last illness, for his sister-in-law recorded that it had to be removed from his sickroom lest it disturb him.

The most musical of Mozart's pets was a starling which he acquired in 1784. He entered its purchase price into an account book he kept as amounting to 34 kreuzer (about $2.50). He also noted, with great delight, that the bird could almost whistle the rondo theme of his newest piano concerto, No. 17 in G, K. 453, which he presumably had been practicing in the room. "*Das war schön*," he wrote in the book of the bird's song—"That was lovely."

The bird lived three years, dying on June 4, 1787. We know the date because Mozart took elaborate note of the occasion.

His Viennese lodging at the time had a garden, and he decided to bury the little creature there. He even composed a set of verses that began: "Here lies a cherished fool, a starling bird," and arranged a funeral procession to which he invited several of his friends. They all joined in singing a bit of music—just what, isn't known. Perhaps Mozart's grief didn't last beyond the day. But it was a better funeral than he himself was to have.

Mozart and Paris

"From Paris the name and fame of a man of great talent resounds through the entire world."

—Leopold Mozart,
letter to Wolfgang,
February 11, 1778

That Mozart and Paris never hit it off well must be an eternal source of regret to those—and surely there are many—who love both the composer and the city. A handful of compositions exist in the Mozart catalogue that are indisputably Parisian, but considering the hopes that went into Mozart's French venture, and the amount of time he devoted to it, the results were disappointingly scanty.

Wolfgang, of course, had spent months in Paris as a child, being admired with his sister as twin musical marvels. This was the Paris, it might be remembered, not only of the Bourbon monarchy, but of Denis Diderot and Jean d'Alembert, the Encyclopedists, whose enlightened rationalism was laying foundations for both modern scientific inquiry and democratic idealism.

Such men (and women, too) were fascinated by the kind of human potential represented by the young Mozarts. Among those particularly responsive to the children was Melchior Grimm, a native of Regensburg in Bavaria, who had settled in Paris where he became a diplomatist and author. Grimm, who knew music, pronounced Wolfgang and Nannerl "*vrais prodiges*" and did all he could to help Leopold obtain court appearances and arrange concerts for the children. After the Mozarts returned home he and Leopold entered into a correspondence that lasted a number of years.

Wolfgang never really wanted to go back to Paris a second time. But by now he was twenty-one years old, and, despite several unquestioned triumphs as a composer, he had not yet been able to obtain a permanent position commensurate with his talent in pay and prestige—a condition that unfortunately was to persist to the end of his life. Leopold Mozart, calculating that if neither Germany nor Italy fully appreciated his son, France certainly would, insisted that he go off to Paris. He would have liked nothing better than to go with him, to manage his attempt to conquer France. Unfortunately his employer, the archbishop of Salzburg, adamantly refused to give him a leave of absence.

Leopold obviously lacked confidence in Wolfgang's capacity, even in his twenties, to make the trip unaided, so he sat down and wrote some fifty letters to Melchior Grimm and other important personages he knew in Paris and along the way, asking them to give his son what assistance they could. Even more important, he ordained that Mozart's mother should travel with him, to provide material comfort, moral support, and helpful advice, and in general to keep him out of trouble.

Wolfgang's reluctance to go was intensified by a romance

in which he became involved en route.* His mother, who was fifty-seven years old and in less than perfect health, had no real stomach for the trip, either. But no one questioned Leopold's authority in such matters, so the two voyagers set out in March 1778.

Wolfgang's stay in Paris, which lasted six months, was a disaster almost from the start. No longer a wunderkind but a young man looking for a job—and a lucrative job at that—he was met with evasions, stalling, inaction, refusals. The one post that was offered to him was that of organist at Versailles; Leopold urged him to take it, pointing out that the pay was good and that he would be close to the king and the court, but Wolfgang, for whatever reasons, said he wasn't interested.

Paris was one of the European cities where the public concert had come into being, though on a limited scale. The Concerts Spirituels had been established in 1725 when an astute impresario observed that the Paris Opéra, or Académie Royale de Musique, as it was known, was closed on religious festival days. He promptly organized orchestral concerts as a substitute, and they quickly received the *spirituel* designation.

Mozart wrote his *Paris* Symphony, No. 31 in D, K. 297, for a Concert Spirituel. The work was enthusiastically applauded, especially because it paid due attention to a device upon which the brilliant Paris orchestra prided itself, the *premier coup d'archet*, the unison opening bow stroke. In a derisive aside to his father, Mozart repeated a joke he had heard in Paris—that at a French concert the last bow stroke was always more welcome than the first.

Altogether in Paris Mozart composed eight works, several of which have been lost. Those that have survived include a

*See "Mozart in Love," page 69.

Anna Maria Mozart, Wolfgang's mother, in her mid-fifties.

ballet score, the charmingly named *Les Petits Riens*, K. 299b, the lovely Sinfonia Concertante for Four Wind Instruments, K. 297b, and, perhaps most Parisian of all, the Flute and Harp Concerto, K. 299, a work to which French performers have been partial ever since and that always sounds especially enchanting in a Parisian setting.

When Mozart and his mother reached Paris after a coach journey of ten days in March of 1778 they took up residence in the Hôtel des Quatre Fils Aymon on the rue de Gros-Chenet (now the rue Sentier) near the Boulevard Poissonnière. Today a commercial district, at the time it was a kind of musical quarter, but then as now it was hardly a fashionable neighborhood.

From these rather dingy surroundings Mozart would sally forth to make his calls, seeking commissions and engagements and giving lessons. Usually his mother remained behind, eating unfamiliar cookery, trying to comprehend a strange and difficult tongue, and in general not finding very much to do except read the advice-filled letters with which her anxious husband bombarded her from his command post in Salzburg.

Anna Maria Mozart has been called the true "heroine of Mozart's life" in a monograph by psychologist Erna Schwerin, published by the Friends of Mozart of New York. Mozart's mother, Schwerin points out, "sacrificed her happiness, comfort, and finally life itself" for her son. Warm, sympathetic, and much given to the earthy humor that characterized the Mozarts' family life, she was an understanding and capable parent at home. But charged as she was with caring for a twenty-one-year-old genius son under the remote control of a dominating and decisive husband, she was bound to end up overwhelmed by her responsibility and frustrated by her circumstances. "He prefers other people to me," she wrote to Leopold even before they had begun the final stages of their trip to the French capital.

Wolfgang's efforts to establish himself in the musical life of Paris were equally frustrating. As many have before and since, he discovered that fashionable audiences were more interested in show than in substance. He was usually received with politeness but seldom with reward and, worst of all, few people really cared about or comprehended his music. He told his father of one visit, to the Duchesse de Chabot, during which he was ushered into an unheated, ice-cold salon and invited to play on a clavier while a "party of gentlemen" sat around in a circle and drew sketches. After first trying to warm up his hands he began to play, but abruptly stopped when he realized no one was paying attention. When he stood up the company, thinking the concert was over, began to applaud and to shower empty compliments upon him. Eager to get out, Mozart told them that the clavier wasn't in very good condition and that he would come back another time. But just then the Duc de Chabot, who was the real music lover in the family, came in, presumably having been delayed elsewhere.

"He sat beside me," Mozart reported in his letter, "and listened with the greatest attention, and I—I forgot the cold and my headache, and in spite of all played the wretched clavier as I play when I am in top form. Give me the best clavier in Europe with an audience who understands nothing, who do not share my feeling for what I am playing, and there is no joy in it for me."

About a month after arriving in Paris, Mozart's mother began to complain of various ailments, including earaches and a sore throat. By the middle of June she was seriously ill and on July 3, 1778, she died. Wolfgang, who had summoned first a German and then a French physician to treat her, was horrified. But he pulled himself together that night to write two letters to Salzburg. The first was to Leopold, telling him only that Anna Maria was "very ill" and concluding "My dear mother is in the hands of the Almighty." The second was to an old family friend, Abbé Joseph Bullinger, telling him the truth and asking him to prepare his father for the sad news. Then, a few days later, Wolfgang sent his father a full account of her illness and death. Anna Maria was buried in the Cemetery of St. Eustache, which seven years later was covered over during an expansion of Les Halles, the great Paris Central Market. The bones of all interred there were removed to the Paris Catacombs, where Anna Maria Mozart presumably still rests.

Following his mother's death, Wolfgang accepted an invitation from Melchior Grimm to move into his dwelling—or rather, that of his mistress, Louise d'Epinay, one of Paris's fashionable liberated women—on the Chaussée d'Antin. It was a most hospitable act, but even in this new and elegant milieu Mozart was unhappy. Grimm was by now a baron, an intellectual who had learned how to make his way in the great world, an art that Mozart never mastered. Grimm wrote to Leopold: "I wish that, for his own good, he had half the talent and twice the ability to handle people (*le double plus d'entregent*)." Grimm and Mme. d'Epinay on one hand and Mozart on the other simply didn't get along very well, and Wolfgang began receiving hints that nobody would much mind if he departed. Grimm went so far as to offer to pay for his return trip to Salzburg, though in the event he actually covered only half the cost.

So in September of 1778 Mozart departed Paris, leaving his dead mother and his shattered hopes behind him. It was a slow and bitter journey that took him back to Salzburg by way of Strasbourg, Mannheim, and Munich. He never returned to Paris, and on many occasions he expressed his aversion for all things French. His letters are dotted with such sentiments as "Let me never hear a Frenchwoman singing Italian operas," "If only the damned French language was not so atrocious for music," and, more comprehensively, "These stupid Frenchmen!"

And yet Paris had had an effect upon him: it was the city in which he grew up to the realities of life, where he faced for the first time personal tragedy and was thrown, unaided, on his own resources. It was a city that tempered and, to an extent, matured him.

It also was a city that—just as Vienna was to do later—never gave him his due while he was alive but subsequently took his music to its heart. But Paris, as it always does, transformed and Gallicized that music and gave it a peculiarly French flair. French performers, right down to our own time, have always had a peculiar affinity for the Flute and Harp Concerto, which musicologist Alfred Einstein describes as "an example of the finest French salon music ... the Andantino is like a François Boucher." A number of French instrumentalists, such as the late pianist Robert Casadesus, have become Mozart specialists. Paris even conferred upon Mozart the distinction of naming a street for him, though it is far from the locale in which he actually lived. French musicologists have contributed notably to Mozart scholarship, particularly in the analyses of his symphonies by Théodore de Wyzewa and Georges de Saint-Foix.

It is perhaps in opera that the French have created, for better or worse, their own Mozartean style. Although Mozart may not have realized it, his music had some admirers in France. One was Marie Antoinette whom—so the story goes—he had once offered to marry when they met as children at the court of Maria Theresa, her mother. She was said to play his piano pieces in her salon at the Trianon. His opera *The Marriage of Figaro*, based on Beaumarchais's pre-Revolutionary play, was popular in Paris. In fact it was performed there in March 1793, a few weeks after the guillotining of King Louis XVI, Marie Antoinette's husband. In true Revolutionary fashion, the work was listed as an *"opéra en cinq actes du Citoyen Mozart."* From the division into five acts it is evident that certain liberties were taken with the score. For the second-act finale, that intricate sequence of interactions among all nine of the opera's principal characters, no fewer than thirty-eight rehearsals were required.

In France this opera has always been called *Les Noces de Figaro* to distinguish it from Beaumarchais's *Le Mariage de Figaro* and also, perhaps, to reflect the Italian *Le nozze di Figaro*. Until quite recently, performances by French companies were likely to be in French translation, with whole sections of the Beaumarchais play being used as spoken dialogue in place of Mozart's recitatives. Only since the French began to stage international festivals, such as that in Aix en Provence in the 1950s, has "Citoyen Mozart" received his due in the form of authentic performances of *Les Noces de Figaro*.

Don Giovanni, usually called *Don Juan* in France, won the approbation of the most famous Frenchman of all, Napoleon Bonaparte. In October 1805, en route to fight the Battle of Austerlitz, Napoleon stopped off at Ludwigsburg and heard a performance of "the German opera *Don Juan*," which, he reported, "seemed very good to me." On the other hand, Napoleon's great literary enemy, Mme. Germaine de Staël, found *Don Giovanni* a bit too rational and intellectual for her, writing in 1813: "This witty alliance of musician and poet also gives a kind of pleasure—but a pleasure that originates in the mind; and this kind of pleasure does not belong to the marvelous sphere of the arts."

Don Giovanni became caught up in the Romantic movement in France, as it did everywhere else, and through the nineteenth century was the most popular of the Mozart operas in Paris. Charles Gounod, the composer of *Faust*, declared it had dominated his life "like a luminous apparition, a kind of revelatory vision." In a typical effusion he declared that if all other music in the world were destroyed it would be possible to reconstruct the entire art from the first-act trio *"Ah, chi mi dice mai"* of Elvira, Don Giovanni, and Leporello.

Performances of *Don Giovanni* in France were almost always in French, and they suffered from the usual indignities heaped upon Mozart's operas in the nineteenth century. The work was turned into a grand opera of Meyerbeerean proportions, with ballets concocted from symphonic minuets and marches, scenes shifted around, and even the *Dies Irae* interpolated into the climactic supper scene. The twentieth century, however, brought about a restoration of the original score, though still with a French text, so that in the celebrated Act I duet *"La ci darem la mano"* Don Juan sang *"Viens, une voix t'appelle,"* and "Zerline" responded: *"Je tremble mais j'écoute."* A *Don Giovanni* in French is not without its special charms.

Of all of Mozart's operas in France, it is *The Magic Flute* that has had the most curious history. Composed by Mozart in 1791, just before his death, it reached Paris in 1801, but so altered that its composer might have had difficulty recognizing his work. Its title was changed to *Les Mystères d'Isis*, its music was assembled from several sources, only some of them Mozartean, by one Ludwig Wenzel Lachnith, and a brand-new text was provided by a literary hack named Étienne Morel. Among other depredations, the second-act quintet and Pamina's aria were replaced by arias lifted bodily from *Don Giovanni* and *La Clemenza di Tito* and transformed into duets. Room was also found for the "Champagne" aria from *Don Giovanni*, except that this was changed into a trio for two sopranos and a bass with the opening words:

> *Heureux délire!*
> *Mon coeur soupire!*

The result, one contemporaneous observer sardonically noted, should have been entitled not *Les Mystères d'Isis* but *Les Misères d'Ici*.

Not until 1865 were the authentic score and libretto of *The Magic Flute* presented in Paris, this time as *La Flute enchantée*, the title by which it has been known in France ever since. Musical tourists of a certain age may remember *La Flute enchantée* as it was performed at the Paris Opéra just before and after World War II—a rather seedy, visually undistinguished production in which Tamino was gotten up like a French prince at the court of Versailles, complete with a powdered wig with a pigtail tied with a little black ribbon, while Sarastro was a youthful Eastern sheikh with a dapper little black beard and waxed moustaches. A French Orientalism pervaded the whole, with the French text adding a layer of elegant artificiality.

In 1954 when the Opéra underwent one of its periodic changes of administration, *La Flute enchantée* was selected, with Rameau's *Les Indes galantes* and Weber's *Oberon*, to symbolize the theater's artistic revitalization. Mozart's work was billed as a "Grand Opéra Féerie" and fitted out with a lavish production that included sixteen scenes and fourteen stage sets and made full use of the theater's elaborate machinery to produce a spectacular fairyland. This was a vision of ancient Egypt as it might have been imagined by an eighteenth-century mind, but the score and text were unadulterated, and the singers were the finest French artists of the day. It had taken a long time, but Paris finally gave Mozart an operatic production that he himself might have enjoyed.

What Mozart Looked Like

"He was a remarkable small man . . ."
—Michael Kelly, *Reminiscences*, 1826

Of all the great composers, Mozart is the only one we should fail to recognize were he suddenly to reappear among us. Bach, Beethoven, Schubert, Brahms, Wagner, Verdi—their faces are reasonably familiar, whether they appear in portraits, plaster busts, or even on T-shirts. Of Mozart alone there is no clear pictorial image, with the result that most modern souvenir busts and other depictions represent an idealized late-eighteenth-century figure of a young man rather than a strongly individualized personality.

Even his friends regarded Mozart as rather nondescript and undistinguished in looks. He had none of the leonine appearance of a Beethoven or the cherubic countenance of a Schubert. He

59

was small in size, somewhat scarred by a childhood bout with smallpox, and had a rather large nose. His most handsome physical characteristic was a shock of fine, light-colored hair, of which he was somewhat vain, since he had it dressed with uncommon frequency. There are one or two references to his eyes being blue, but most observers, even while giving physical descriptions, fail to mention eye color at all, so some doubt exists on the subject. Apparently his eye coloration was not very striking. He never seems to have worn spectacles. He had a tenor voice, which is somewhat ironic in view of the fact that operatic baritones have had no better friend, as evidenced by the title roles of *Don Giovanni* and *The Marriage of Figaro*.

Mozart's unprepossessing appearance as an adult is in striking contrast to his attractiveness as a child, which was commented upon by dozens of observers who have left accounts of his European tours as a wunderkind. He carried off his prodigious childhood talent with a naturalness that charmed his listeners everywhere. "The boy is handsome, vivacious, graceful, and full of good manners," wrote Johann Adolf Hasse, himself a famous opera composer, when he heard Wolfgang play in Vienna at the age of thirteen. For some reason Mozart's rate of growth slowed up during his teens; his physical development did not keep pace with that of his sister Nannerl.

As Wolfgang grew older he developed a philosophical attitude toward his slight physique. There is a note of humorous ruefulness in the way he closes a letter written from Rome to his mother and sister at the age of fourteen:

> I have had the honor of kissing St. Peter's foot in
> St. Peter's church and, as I have the misfortune to be
> so small, I, that same old dunce,
>
> > *Wolfgang Mozart*
> > had to be lifted up.

Johann Nepomuk della Croce's portrait of the Mozart family.
Wolfgang's mother, who had died, is shown in portrait on wall.

When he was twenty-one he wrote, this time with bitterness, after meeting the civic and musical authorities of the town of Mannheim: "They probably think that because I am little and young, that nothing mature or great can come out of me, but they will soon see."

In some reminiscences written by Nannerl Mozart a year after her brother's death she describes him as "small, thin, pale in color and entirely lacking in any pretensions as to physiognomy and bodily appearance." A similar description was left by the German writer Ludwig Tieck, who in his old age remembered going into an empty theater in 1789 just before the performance of an opera and seeing "an unprepossessing figure in a gray overcoat" moving about the orchestra pit examining the music on each stand. He entered into a conversation with the gray-clad man in the course of which he told him how much he admired Mozart's operas. "That is very good of you, young man," was the reply. Only later did Tieck realize he had been talking to Mozart himself.

Of course, there were plenty of observers on whom the dominant impression left by Mozart was not his size but his animation, bright conversation, humor, and particularly the radiance that seemed to possess him when he was playing his music. Michael Kelly, a young Irish tenor who was a particular friend of Wolfgang for several years in Vienna, reported fully on his physical slightness and paleness. However, when music was involved, says Kelly, Mozart's countenance "lighted up with the glowing rays of genius—it is as impossible to describe it as it would be to paint sunbeams."

At least nine authentic portraits of Mozart were made during his lifetime and have been preserved; the trouble is that no two of them really look alike. The most striking in conveying some sense of inward vigor and intensity is that showing him at age twenty-one wearing the decoration of the Order of the Golden Spur, the dignity conferred on him by Pope Clement XIV. This portrait of the dignified young musician, his hand thrust into his waistcoat, was by an artist whose name has been lost, but Mozart's family called it "completely lifelike."

A sense of accuracy also is conveyed by the appearance of Mozart in a family portrait made in oil by Johann Nepomuk della Croce in Salzburg in 1780, when Wolfgang was approaching twenty-five. His mother had died eighteen months before, so she is represented by a portrait hanging on the wall. Of the three remaining members of the family, Wolfgang and Nannerl are depicted seated at the keyboard, she playing the treble, he the bass, with his right hand crossed over her left, while Leopold, looking thin and wan, holds his violin propped upon the piano. After Wolfgang's death a distinguished artist named Barbara

Krafft was commissioned to paint his picture for inclusion in a Vienna gallery of composers. Krafft copied Mozart's likeness from the family portrait, and also had the benefit of consultations with Nannerl Mozart.

Perhaps the best-known Mozart portrait is that begun in 1782 by Joseph Lange, Mozart's brother-in-law. Lange was an actor who painted only as a sideline, but the picture, the lower right-hand corner of which he never finished, shows a certain amount of skill and a sympathetic feeling. But it has little connection to the other portraits. The face of the twenty-six-year-old composer, shown in profile, is plump, and his full head of hair is certainly in evidence. Yet the expression seems somewhat vacant, and very little sense of personality comes through. Lange's portrait, like most of the others, raises the possibility that no artist of the time, no matter how great his capacities, when confronted by a rather ordinary-looking human being, was able to capture the characteristics that were uniquely Mozart's.

The Scatological Mozart

"Regards to the whole company of shitters!"

—Mozart, letter to his father,
October 31, 1777

ohn Ruskin, that rather severe moralist, once attempted to draw a distinction between "simple and innocent vulgarity," which he ascribed to "untrained and undeveloped bluntness of mind and body," and "true, inbred vulgarity" which, he feared, could lead to bestiality and crime.

The Mozart family, Wolfgang included, seems to have had more than its share of the former variety. It surfaces most prominently in their letters, which abound in coarse and ribald expressions and sentiments. True, the family was writing for itself and not for outsiders, although Leopold Mozart did suggest, at one point, that all letters be saved, with the idea that he might one day publish a biography of his brilliant son. In any case, no one felt any inhibitions.

The earthy, vulgar boisterousness of the letters represented both a regional and family tradition. Salzburgers in general had a reputation for grossness of speech; devout Catholics that they were, they distinguished between blasphemy and mere obscenity. The Mozart family in particular seemed to enjoy talking dirty, using blunt, peasant terminology, and telling off-color jokes. Why else would Anna Maria Mozart have written good-humoredly to her husband "Keep well my love. Into your mouth your arse you'll shove"—a little ditty that evidently was popular in the family, for Wolfgang later repeated it in some of *his* letters. All four of the Mozarts indulged in similar linguistic heartiness, especially when referring to bodily functions, although Leopold and Nannerl usually were a bit more restrained than Wolfgang and his mother.

Occasionally Mozart used expletives to vent his anger, as when he dismissed both the city of Salzburg and its ruling prince-archbishop with the comprehensive comment: "I shit on both of them." For the most part, however, graphic language was reserved for humorous effect, and it dealt mainly with defecation, breaking wind, and similar acts usually unmentioned in polite society.

The fullest flowering—if that is the word—of Mozartean scatology occurred in a series of letters Wolfgang wrote to his cousin Maria Anna Thekla, daughter of Leopold's younger brother Franz Aloys Mozart, a bookbinder in Augsburg. They had known each other as children, but he was twenty-one and she nineteen when they began to correspond, and they quickly found they shared a taste for bawdy horseplay and toilet humor. Inasmuch as they also visited each other from time to time, some suspicion has arisen that their relationship may have gone further, but

Wolfgang once told his father that he was a virgin until marriage and no actual evidence to the contrary has ever been produced.

However, Mozart and his cousin, who bore the nickname of "Bäsle," or "Little Cousin," certainly indulged themselves to the full by writing obscene and suggestive letters to each other, a typical Wolfgangian sign-off being "W. A. Mozart, who shits without a fart." Maria Anna Thekla, incidentally, appears to have led a merry enough life after her correspondence with her famous cousin ceased. She lived to the age of eighty-three and, while she never married, became the mistress of a village postmaster and bore him an illegitimate daughter named Marianna Viktoria Mozart, who died in 1857.

Maria Anna Thekla Mozart, the "Little Cousin" to whom Wolfgang wrote ribald letters.

The scatological aspect of Mozart's correspondence, though known to scholars, was left unmentioned during the Victorian era. Such terms were deemed inappropriate for music-lovers of the time, particularly since they were so much at odds with the accepted image of Mozart as a kind of Dresden-china figurine. It was not until the British author Emily Anderson published her magnificent three-volume English translation of the Mozart family letters in 1938 that British and American readers became aware of this hitherto unknown side of Mozart's character. In a typical review, the weekly book supplement of the *New York Herald Tribune*, while lavishly praising the collection, warned readers that some of the letters were "of a grossness rarely duplicated outside of Martial and Rabelais."

Actually, Mozart's letters toned down considerably in their boisterousness as he grew older; his mother, who had shared his gusty taste in correspondence, was dead, and he was no longer interested in his "little cousin." Nevertheless, a curious reversion to his erotic epistolary style occurred in at least one letter written at the age of thirty-three to his wife Constanze. Mozart was in Berlin preparing to return home from a trip, and in a letter dated May 23, 1789, he describes having an erection as he anticipates his reunion with her. Some of the words in the letter have been blotted out by a later hand (presumably that of Constanze's second husband Georg Nikolaus von Nissen) but the meaning is clear enough: "Arrange your sweet nest daintily, for my little fellow deserves it indeed; he has really behaved himself very well and is only longing to possess your sweetest. . . ."

Since virtually everything Mozart touched turned to music, it is no surprise to find him composing, from time to time, vocal pieces to ribald texts. These canons and songs were written mainly for home performance to amuse Mozart and his friends.

Today they are principally encountered on recordings; in fact about twenty years ago Epic Records issued an English-language version of some of them under the feeble title "Wolfgang Amadeus Mozart Is a Dirty Old Man." One of the best-known of these vocal pieces is "*O du eselhafter Martin*," a canon apparently addressed affectionately to an impresario friend, Philipp Martin. It invites the "silly-assed" Martin to "kiss me, kiss me, kiss me, right now in the behind." Several other songs are even more graphic in their instructions. Mozart never found it a paradox to express himself in music with the utmost refinement and subtlety and in words with total freedom and frankness. In music he stood among the giants, in everyday life he was one of the boys.

Mozart in Love

"If I had to marry every girl with whom I've flirted, I should have had at least 200 wives."

Mozart, letter to his father,
July 25, 1781

The very first letter Mozart ever wrote—or at least the first to have been preserved—was sent at the age of thirteen to an unidentified girlfriend in Salzburg. She had dared him to write her something in Latin, and he did so by copying a sentence from a textbook and, in turn, challenging her to translate it. He wrote frequently to girls while away on his travels throughout his adolescence, and when he didn't correspond with them directly would ask his sister to convey his greetings. "Please give my regards to Jungfrau Mitzerl," he wrote to Nannerl, "and tell her she must never doubt my love."

Jungfrau Mitzerl was the Mozarts' next-door neighbor in Salzburg, and Wolfgang was eighteen at the time. On another occasion he archly asked Nannerl to give his salutations to "you know who," and when he didn't have anybody in particular in mind simply sent regards to all "pretty girls and Fräuleins."

Mozart also met attractive young women on his travels. Young sopranos interested him particularly. In Munich he was enchanted at the opera by a Mademoiselle Kaiser who, he wrote to his father, was "the daughter of a cook by a count and a very attractive girl." He was so delighted with her appearance and her singing alike that for a time he was fired with a desire "to advance the cause of the German stage."

However, it was not until Wolfgang was twenty-one and visiting Mannheim on his way to Paris with his mother that he really fell head over heels in love for the first time. As it turned out, it was a romance that, although it brought bitterness in the end, exerted a considerable influence upon the course of his life.

Mannheim, with a population of about 25,000—about twice that of Salzburg—was known as the "paradise of musicians," chiefly because of the excellence of its court orchestra, which some thought was the best in Europe. Mozart and his mother spent four months in Mannheim, starting October 30, 1777. By now he was a composer of unmistakable accomplishments; he had already written the opera *La finta giardiniera* (*The Pretended Garden Girl*), a charming comedy that proved the hit of the Munich Carnival of 1775, and the Piano Concerto No. 9 in E-flat, K. 271, the first of his great works in this form.

Mozart had stopped off in Mannheim with the idea that he might obtain a permanent post from Elector Carl Theodor (Elector was the title given those German princes who were entitled to participate in the election of the Holy Roman Emperor). As it turned out, he didn't get the job, but he did meet a girl.

Her name was Aloysia Weber and she was one of four sisters. Her father, Fridolin Weber, earned a scanty living as a part-time singer, copyist, and prompter at the opera; her mother, Maria Cäcilie, rented rooms and was ever on the lookout for advantageous marriages for her daughters Josepha, Aloysia, Constanze, and Sophie. Of the family's musical propensities there was no doubt; Fridolin Weber's brother Franz Anton was to become the father of the composer Carl Maria von Weber, born in 1786.

Aloysia Weber, the second daughter, was sixteen years old, physically attractive, and the possessor of a beautiful soprano voice. Mozart was enchanted. He wrote arias for her to sing, tutored her in style and interpretation, worked hours with her at the piano. Leopold had wanted him to proceed to Paris immediately if he couldn't get a post at the elector's court, but Mozart, smitten with Aloysia, thought of all sorts of excuses to prolong his stay in Mannheim. He even wrote to Leopold proposing that he abandon the Paris trip altogether and travel instead with the Weber family to Italy where, he argued, he might further both his and Aloysia's careers. He also offered to bring her and the entire Weber clan back to Salzburg so Leopold could meet them all; of Aloysia he wrote: "As far as her singing is concerned, I would wager my life that she will bring me renown."

Leopold, of course, was beside himself at thus seeing his plans for his son's advancement frustrated. He wrote to Wolfgang at great length of his "amazement and horror" at the thought of his traipsing around Italy with the Webers and being "captured by some woman" instead of fulfilling his destiny. Speaking of the cities and towns on Wolfgang's projected itinerary with Aloysia, Leopold said: "Those are places for lesser lights, half-composers, scribblers, fakers! Name me one great composer who would deign to take so abject a step. Off with

Aloysia Weber as she appeared in Grétry's opera *Zémire et Azor*.

you to Paris, and that quickly! Find your place among the great. *Aut Caesar aut nihil!*"

Bombarded with such admonitions, Mozart had little choice. His mother, who played a curiously neutral role in this family crisis, was resigned to going to Paris even though she had little desire for the trip. She, too, rarely argued with Leopold. Wolfgang presumably felt the first stirrings of unrest against his father during the dispute, but he was not yet ready for open revolt. He bade a bitter farewell to the Webers and left with his mother for France. But he continued to write to Aloysia.

Considering the misfortunes that befell Mozart in Paris, a voyage to Italy with the Webers might not have had the dire effects that Leopold anticipated. But on the other hand it probably would not have led to a union with Aloysia Weber either. With her charms, both personal and musical, she was in a position to play the field, and she did. From her standpoint their romance looked far less promising than from Wolfgang's. She was a beautiful girl on the threshhold of a great career; he was an undersized youth who had barely begun to shave, and a composer in search of a job. Neither in looks nor in prospects did he rank as the pick of the crop among her numerous suitors.

When Mozart returned from his fruitless and tragic half year in Paris, he met Aloysia and her family in Munich on his way back to Salzburg. By now she had achieved considerable standing as a singer at the opera, and she had completely lost interest in her erstwhile tutor. Wolfgang was wearing a red coat with black buttons and a black arm band, proper mourning dress in the Parisian style. Aloysia considered this a rather ridiculous costume—almost like livery. Although we have no record of her actual words, she made it clear to him that she had decided to terminate their little romance. Wolfgang, so the story goes, promptly sat down at the piano and sang a little ditty that began: "I gladly leave that maiden that will not have me." Some accounts add that his song wound up: *"Leck mir das Mensch in Arsch das mich nicht will"*—"Anyone who doesn't like me can lick my ass."

It was a flippant farewell, but it didn't measure the depth of his true feelings, for immediately afterward he wrote to his father—without, however, telling him the true cause of his misery—"Today I can only weep."

Mozart in Salzburg

"Salzburg is no place for my talent."

—Mozart, letter to the Abbé Bullinger,
August 7, 1778

Few cities have turned a native son into an industry as successfully as Salzburg has with Mozart. A statue of him, erected fifty years after his death, adorns the main square; his two residences are still preserved and one has been turned into a museum; the chief musical institution in the town is called the Mozarteum; every summer since 1917 a great festival is devoted to his works. The shops are filled with Mozart statuettes, ashtrays, beer mugs, portraits, postcards, candy, and other souvenirs.

Yet Mozart hated Salzburg passionately, took every opportunity he could to travel elsewhere, and, after he made his final break, returned only once for a visit.

Salzburg today is a city of over 100,000, but in Mozart's time it was a town of barely 10,000. It was thoroughly Roman Catholic; the entire Protestant population of the region had been banished (though they were permitted to leave gradually and unharmed) a quarter of a century before Mozart's birth.

The region was ruled by a prince-archbishop who drew his authority concurrently from the Holy Roman Emperor and the pope. The prince-archbishop who expelled the Protestants was Leopold von Firmian, but in 1756, when Mozart was born, he had been succeeded by the somewhat more tolerant Count Sigismund Schrattenbach.

Like most princely rulers of his era, Schrattenbach maintained a musical establishment—one of the signs of a cultivated and enlightened court in the eighteenth century. It numbered around 100, including an orchestra of 33, a choir of 30 adults and 15 boys, and various other performers. One of its leading members was Michael Haydn (younger brother of Joseph Haydn), who held the rank of conductor of the orchestra. Most of Mozart's friends in Salzburg were drawn from this musical group, including Andreas Schachtner, a trumpeter and fiddler, who was a particular favorite of Wolfgang as a child.

As long as Sigismund Schrattenbach was Archbishop, the Salzburg musical organization ran along fairly contentedly, though it never became more than a provincial establishment. Schrattenbach quickly became aware of Mozart's extraordinary talents, although he suspected that Leopold might have had something to do with the young genius's early compositions. Leopold always denied that he in any way polished or improved upon his son's work.

According to one story, Schrattenbach was so skeptical that he actually shut Wolfgang into a private apartment for several days and set him to composing a cantata, without coming into contact with his father or anybody else who could help him. Mozart, who was ten years old at the time, passed the test successfully. Even more important, Schrattenbach permitted both Mozarts to travel pretty much at will to the various cities to which they had been invited, although he usually took care to suspend Leopold's salary as Vice Kapellmeister during such expeditions.

Schrattenbach died in 1771, and when the time came to select his successor, Mozart encountered the first of the numerous strokes of bad luck that were to dog him throughout his life. A leading candidate for the post was the bishop of Chiemsee, Count Ferdinand Christoph von Zeill, a musical connoisseur and an early admirer of Mozart. However, he withdrew in favor of an opposing contender, Hieronymus, Count von Colloredo, who bore the not very distinguished (or euphonious) title of Bishop of Gurk and who had a reputation as a martinet.

Had Zeill been chosen archbishop, Wolfgang's life might well have been easier. The forty-year-old Colloredo proved to be a most unpleasant overlord not only for the Mozarts but for most other Salzburgers. The populace as a whole had openly favored the candidacy of Zeill, which hardly endeared them to the new archbishop. On the day of Colloredo's induction the townspeople stood in the streets in silence as the procession went by. One eyewitness recorded: "It was a fair day. An urchin in the midst of the onlookers shouted 'Hurrah!' and was promptly given a box on the ears by a merchant who said: 'Boy, dost thou shout while the people weep?' "

The problem seems to have been that the prince-archbishop, while professing to be a man of enlightened thought whose favorite author was Voltaire, in actuality was a thoroughgoing aristocrat with little regard for common people. Although Colloredo was well-read and a fair musician (he actually sat in as a violinist in the court orchestra from time to time), he was disdainful toward his hirelings and never rose above the notion held by much of the eighteenth-century nobility that musicians were on the same plane as domestic servants and should be dealt with as such.

Colloredo's musical arrangements were also shaped by his preference, shared by the Hapsburgs in general, for Italians rather than Germans, Austrians, Hungarians, or Czechs. Colloredo, himself of Italian stock, knew that Leopold Mozart was aching to be named Kapellmeister and was well qualified for the position; instead he appointed Domenico Fischietti, a Neapolitan who had formerly served in Dresden. His favorite singer was the castrato Francesco Ceccarelli. He even is alleged to have remarked that Wolfgang really did not know enough about composing and ought to go to Naples for further study!

Actually, the relations between the new archbishop and his resident prodigy seem to have begun fairly well. Colloredo gave Wolfgang, then sixteen years old, the title of Konzertmeister with a modest salary of 150 gulden (about \$750); he also permitted him a short leave of absence for a trip to Italy. Even more important, he gave him several musical commissions, including a "dramatic serenade" to be performed at his installation. This proved to be *Il Sogno di Scipione* (*The Dream of Scipio*), about a noble Roman contending with symbolic characters named Constancy and Fortune. It was strictly a *pièce d'occasion* and has the distinction today of being perhaps the least performed of all of Mozart's stage works. Something about Colloredo did not bring out the best in Mozart, although he composed a number of fresh-sounding church works for performance in Salzburg, including several short masses and the brilliant motet "*Exsultate, jubilate*" (K. 165), which remains a favorite soprano showpiece to this day.

Hieronymus, Count of Colloredo, painted in his ecclesiastical vestments.

But none of this really satisfied Wolfgang, who had seen too many other cities and heard too much music elsewhere to be content to remain in Salzburg. Even Leopold realized that his son's stimulation came when he was permitted to travel and accept commissions in larger and more cosmopolitan cities. Salzburg simply offered insufficient scope in which to exercise his talents. There was no opera, the orchestra was hardly at his disposal (as was Joseph Haydn's orchestra at Esterháza), and the archbishop made it clear that, while he liked music, he didn't like too much of it—for instance, he set a limit of forty-five minutes' duration for church pieces.

In his efforts to get away, Wolfgang tried for permanent posts in Vienna, Munich, Mannheim, and Paris, but nobody wanted a now-overaged prodigy, particularly one whose personal flair was minimal and whose music did not always fit within conventional molds. Mozart kept writing home optimistically, telling of encouraging words spoken to him by one courtier or another, but Leopold, more worldly wise, received such reports skeptically. In Munich, Wolfgang reported, the elector had told him: "Yes, my dear boy, but I have no vacancy. . . . If only there were a vacancy." To which Leopold replied: "I prefer merchants or other honest people to these courtiers!"

Some of the Mozarts' correspondence was carried on in code, for they feared that Colloredo might be opening their mail. The code consisted of a simple substitution of certain letters of the alphabet for certain others. It would hardly have fooled even an amateur cryptologist; nevertheless it gave them a feeling of security. Whether the archbishop actually stooped to intercepting and reading their mail is not known, but that they thought him capable of it surely indicated the regard in which they held him.

The Mozarts had many friends in Salzburg. Particularly in his childhood Wolfgang enjoyed the affection of Lorenz Hagenauer, Leopold's landlord and banker; Schachtner the trumpeter; Abbé Bullinger to whom he wrote so despairingly following his mother's death in Paris; and others attached either to the court or to the musical establishment. Similarly, the Mozart household itself was warm in feeling and close-knit in interests;

it was not for many years that the rift between Mozart and his father developed. Indeed Mozart, whether in his parents' home in Salzburg or in his own married life later in Vienna, must go down with Bach and Mendelssohn as one of the great family men of musical history. In contrast to Handel, Beethoven, and Brahms, all of whom lived and died bachelors, they demonstrated the compatibility of familial and artistic life.

Though Mozart became an expert billiard player and enjoyed dancing, he never had any strong inclination toward recreation for its own sake. Despite his widespread travels, tourism as such was of little interest; though he passed through some of Europe's most spectacular scenery and significant historical sites, he scarcely gave them a mention in his correspondence.

The principal—and rather startling—home diversion of the Mozart family was *Bölzelschiessen*, shooting at targets with air-guns. They and their friends would have regular contests, meeting at different houses on Sunday afternoons. The targets were home-made and usually consisted of a picture accompanied by some verses. Apparently the guns fired darts rather than bullets. Small cash awards of a few kreuzer were set aside for the best marksmen of the day, and if anyone were absent another member of the group was permitted to take his turn in the shooting. Both men and women participated and exact scores were kept. After Mozart and his mother left for their trip to Paris, both continued to be represented in the shooting, and Leopold kept them informed as to their winnings and losings. The family also played piquet and other card games, walked Bimperl the dog, visited the neighbors, and engaged in the thousand other activities that nobody bothers to record yet that make up the fabric of daily life.

With three musicians—Leopold, Wolfgang, and Nannerl— in the family, the Mozarts' rooms were frequently the site of impromptu recitals or practice sessions for ensembles of various sizes and combinations. Even as a child, Wolfgang joined in these, playing either the violin or the clavier. The quality of his home life was never among his complaints. With a more amiable archbishop, more recognition of his talent, and more freedom to travel for both himself and his father, it is conceivable that Wolfgang would have been less restless in Salzburg, although his eventual departure would have been inevitable.

In any event, as he entered his twenties he was heartily sick of the place and expressed his desire to cut his ties to Salzburg and its archbishop alike. But since he was officially in service to the court, he had to formally ask permission to depart, and he had to do so delicately lest he injure his worried father's position. Accordingly he wrote a properly deferential letter to "Your Grace, Most Worthy Prince of the Holy Roman Empire" —how its obsequious language must have rankled him!— requesting "most humbly" a discharge from his duties in Salzburg. Among other things, he pointed out that "the Gospel teaches us to use our talents" to contribute to family support as well as to advance individual talents. After due deliberation, Colloredo condescendingly gave his permission, though he couldn't resist a parting gibe by picking up Mozart's reference to the Gospel and replying that "in the name of the Gospel both father and son have my permission to seek their fortune elsewhere." There may have been an implied threat in this, for Leopold had no intention of leaving and only Wolfgang actually departed on the journey to Mannheim and Paris. However much he detested Colloredo, Leopold remained loyal to the end of his life.

Perhaps it was as well that he did, for when Wolfgang returned from the debacle in Paris, with his mother dead, his romance over, and no sign of a job in sight, Leopold was able to convince the archbishop that he should take his son back into his service. Accordingly Colloredo offered him the post of court and cathedral organist with an annual salary of 450 gulden (about $2,250). Wolfgang reluctantly accepted and for two years played at Salzburg church functions. During this time he also somehow managed to produce two of his enduring masterpieces, the opera *Idomeneo*, written for performance at Munich, where it was a considerable success, and the Sinfonia Concertante for Violin and Viola, K. 364, a dark-hued masterpiece that remains one of the jewels of the concerto literature.

But even such creations, and the accolades they received, failed to convince Colloredo that he had in his employ a musical genius. To his grace Wolfgang was an impertinent and unruly young man; and the archbishop treated him accordingly with the disdain and disregard he accorded his other servants, particularly the less satisfactory ones.

In Salzburg Wolfgang's family provided something of a cushion against the petty humiliations that went with his job. At least he lived and dined in his own home, although he was always on call. But when the archbishop went a-traveling Wolfgang was put in a place at the tail end of his entourage. He was assigned to the servants' table at meals and in general found his freedom severely curtailed.

The unhappy story came to a climax in 1781, when Mozart was twenty-five. He was peremptorily ordered to Vienna, where Colloredo had gone for the latter part of the winter. Wolfgang had no objections to spending some time in Vienna, but when he arrived there he found that instead of being permitted to take independent lodgings, like several other members of the archbishop's entourage, he was expected to live in the house where Colloredo himself stayed with his domestic staff.

At mealtimes, Wolfgang wrote to his father, "the two valets sit at the head of the table, but at least I have the honor of being placed above the cooks. . . . As soon as I finish my lunch, I get up and go." It is possible that Wolfgang was a bit of a snob himself, but he knew his own worth and he also knew that he was regarded as a celebrity by practically everyone except his own employer.

What disturbed Wolfgang even more than his lowly position at the table was that the archbishop did everything he could to prevent him from performing music for anyone besides himself while in Vienna. Other members of the nobility invited him to play at their homes—which conceivably could mean a substantial gift—but Colloredo declined to grant permission. On one occasion, Wolfgang reported to Leopold, he could have earned half his annual pay by appearing at an entertainment for Emperor Joseph II, but Colloredo, who had scheduled a party himself that night, wouldn't release him. The archbishop even declined to let Mozart play at a charity concert for the widows of Vienna's musicians—a mean-spirited act that provoked such an outcry of protests that Colloredo was forced to rescind it.

The ultimate break could have come over a dozen issues, but, as so often happens, it was triggered by a relatively trivial dispute—whether Wolfgang would leave Vienna for the return trip to Salzburg by the Wednesday or the Saturday coach. The archbishop insisted on Wednesday; he said he had a package he wished Mozart to carry home for him. Mozart forbore to tell the archbishop that he could carry his own package, but he insisted that he couldn't leave before Saturday. The archbishop, according to Mozart, cried: "There is the door; I will have nothing more to do with such a villain." "Nor I with you," Mozart said he replied.

Leopold Mozart, who by now had probably despaired of Wolfgang's ability to gain a position anywhere but in Salzburg, and who understandably had begun to fear for his own job there, beseeched his son to reconsider, to apologize to the archbishop, to apply for reinstatement. He presumably also sensed that the break was at hand, that if Wolfgang stayed in Vienna it would be forever, and that their long years of trust and intimacy had ended. Wolfgang must have shared this realization, but this time he was determined not to go back.

If he had, there is little doubt that the archbishop would once more have taken him in, for when Wolfgang tried to present a written resignation at Colloredo's residence he was several times turned away with the paper still in his hand. Finally he was so insistent that Count Georg Anton Felix Arco, chief chamberlain to the archbishop, accepted the resignation on behalf of his master. Furthermore, he added injury to insult by actually propelling Mozart out the door with a kick in the behind. Thus did Salzburg say farewell to its most illustrious son, and Hieronymus, Count of Colloredo, write his name into history.

Early Mozart

"I am unable to toss off inferior stuff."

—Mozart, letter to his father,
July 31, 1782

What kind of music had Mozart composed by the time
he left Salzburg for good at the age of twenty-five?
In numbers, he had written more than 350 works, from brief
piano pieces to full operas, including the music he composed
in childhood. As a composer, no less than as a performer, he
was one of the most astonishing prodigies who ever lived.

And yet he was not *the* most astonishing. That distinction
belongs to Felix Mendelssohn, a member of the next generation
who produced such works as the Octet in E-flat for Strings at
age sixteen and the *Midsummer Night's Dream* Overture at seventeen, both of which surpassed in quality anything that Mozart
wrote in his teen years.

Yet Mozart's early work as a body remains a remarkable achievement, and when he left Salzburg it was as a fully mature composer with several works of genius already behind him. Efforts are sometimes made to exculpate the shabby-souled Hieronymus Colloredo on the grounds that the really great Mozart had not emerged in Salzburg. That is true only in a narrow sense; Mozart (unlike Mendelssohn) kept growing in mastery throughout his short life. But there were many wonderful achievements in his Salzburg years that should have been recognized by a musical connoisseur such as the cultivated archbishop professed to be.

While many of Mozart's earliest childhood pieces possess a certain charm, we listen to them today mainly because they are by Mozart. It is fascinating to follow his development from a proficient imitator of the prevailing musical styles to a profoundly original and imaginative creator. And from the time of his Paris trip—that is, from the age of twenty onward—the intimations of immortality become increasingly evident.

Several of Mozart's Parisian compositions, as already noted, remain active in today's repertory. So do several of the serenades and divertissements he wrote in Salzburg, including the *Haffner* Serenade (K. 250), written on the occasion of the wedding of a family friend, and the *Serenata Notturna* (K. 239), an enchanting work for a double orchestra. There were no fewer than five violin concertos which are still eagerly performed by modern violinists, as well as a number of church pieces which audiences today find worth hearing even if Mozart's archbishop did not. These are all in addition to such previously mentioned pieces as the Piano Concerto No. 9 in E-flat and the Sinfonia Concertante for Violin and Viola.

And then there were the operas. Mozart wrote his first aria (for tenor) at the age of nine while in London; he collaborated, at eleven, with two other Salzburg musicians in composing an oratorio; and at the same age wrote *Apollo and Hyacinthus*, an "intermezzo"—actually a short semi-operatic piece for presentation in the interval of a play at Salzburg University.

Carried away by his son's youthful successes, Leopold Mozart succeeded in persuading Emperor Joseph II that Wolfgang, who by now had reached the ripe age of twelve, should be commissioned to compose an opera for presentation in Vienna. The resultant work, based on a Goldoni play, was called *La finta semplice* (*The Pretended Simpleton*) and was about two pairs of lovers who succeed in their marriage plans by outwitting two old men trying to thwart them. Unfortunately for Leopold (and Wolfgang), the project ran into opposition at the Viennese court and the production never came off, though, as a kind of consolation prize, the work was later performed at Salzburg with the approval of the then archbishop, Sigismund Schrattenbach.

Leopold Mozart was forever blaming the intrigues of rival composers for the problems Wolfgang so often encountered in getting his operas performed. Undoubtedly anti-Mozart cabals did exist, for jealousies were rampant in eighteenth-century Austrian musical circles—not that they have been any less so in other times, including our own.

But Wolfgang's youth also contributed to the opposition he met, as has been particularly well documented by the case of his opera *Mitridate, rè di Ponto*, composed two years after *La finta semplice*. If an American opera house today were suddenly to announce that it had commissioned a fourteen-year-old boy to write an opera to open its season, great would be the consternation thereby produced. Singers would grumble, orchestral players express skepticism, subscribers raise their eyebrows. Indeed, a general protest might be heard to the effect that the management would be better off spending its money for something else.

All these reactions are exactly what took place in 1770 when the Royal Ducal Theater of Milan (which later became La Scala) signed a contract with Wolfgang commissioning *Mitridate* for the opening of its carnival season on the night after Christmas. Nearly everybody connected with the opera house was in revolt, but the opera had to be mounted since it had been ordered staged by the governor general of Lombardy, Count Karl Joseph Firmian, who was fascinated by young Mozart and was determined to see whether he could actually compose an entire dramatic opera.

Wolfgang was given no choice as to subject matter—he was simply handed a libretto, based on Racine's classic play about Mithridates, king of Pontus, who is tormented by the mistaken belief that his sons are disloyal and his wife unfaithful. He was also given no choice as to singers; and to make matters worse, he had to wait to consult with them before actually composing the arias they were to sing.

To pass the time in Milan, he decided to compose the recitatives—those long sing-song passages of conversation—in advance. In a letter home he said: "My dear Mamma, I cannot write much, for my fingers ache from composing so many recitatives. Mamma, I beg you to pray for me, that my opera may go well and that we may be happy together again." While working on *Mitridate* he had several other events to report: he took a ride on a donkey, underwent an operation for an abscessed tooth, noticed that his voice was beginning to break. In at least a few respects, then, Mozart's childhood was fairly normal.

A few of the singers, when they arrived, made the inevitable complaints about singing music by a fourteen-year-old. But most, including the *castrato* who performed the title role, were delighted. In fact, Leopold Mozart reported to his wife that "the prima donna and primo uomo are simply enchanted with their duet" and added: "The primo uomo has actually said that if this duet does not go over, he will let himself be castrated again!"

The audience was equally ecstatic. Leopold wrote proudly home how the audience had cried "Long live the little Maestro!" as they cheered the young composer, clad in a scarlet suit trimmed with gold braid and lined with sky-blue satin.

Wolfgang had other youthful operatic successes. His charming *Bastien and Bastienne*, a short pastoral piece with simple, graceful arias linked by spoken passages, was performed in the garden of the Vienna home of Dr. Mesmer, the celebrated experimenter in hypnotism, or, as it was called by some, "mesmerism." Mozart's overture to this little work still startles listeners by the uncanny resemblance of its opening notes to the main theme of Beethoven's *Eroica* Symphony, written thirty-seven years later.

For all their lovely moments, Mozart's early operas would have faded into oblivion were it not for their authorship. Indeed, aside from an aria or two, they *did* fade into oblivion for decades, for it has only been during the twentieth century—and the late twentieth century at that—that musicologists have written learnedly about *Mitridate, Ascanio in Alba, Il Sogno di Scipione, Lucio Silla, La finta giardiniera, Il Rè pastore* and others. These works have now been all recorded, and some are occasionally performed, and each in its way offers a foretaste of the marvels that were to follow.

The first of Mozart's genuinely mature operas was *Idomeneo, rè di Creta*, which he composed when he was twenty-four. It was commissioned for a performance in Munich by the elector of Mannheim, largely as the result of the persuasion of several singers and instrumentalists in the town who liked and admired Mozart.

Idomeneo is about a legendary King of Crete, a participant in the Trojan War, who, like Jephthah in the Book of Judges, vows to sacrifice the first living being he sees in gratitude to the deity after a safe return from peril, only to find it is his own child he must kill. *Idomeneo* has had one of the most curious histories of all of Mozart's operas. It was written—like *Mitridate*—in a form, *opera seria*, that belonged to a previous era and was already on the way out: a series of individual arias linked by recitative, with only an occasional duet or ensemble. Once again, it posed the challenge to Mozart of working together with singers and putting up with their vagaries. The title role was sung by Anton Raaff, a sixty-five-year-old tenor whose voice was worn out, while that of Idamante, the king's son, was entrusted to an inexperienced and clumsy young *castrato*, Vincenzo dal Prato. Mozart managed to give old Raaff music he could sing effectively without too much strain, and he jollied the younger man, whom he jocularly referred to in his letters home as "*mio molto amato castrato dal Prato*" ("my much beloved *castrato* dal Prato"), into giving the performance of his life.*

Idomeneo was a success, as indeed it should have been, for it contains some extraordinary music, including a quartet in which the king sends away his son in an effort to avoid carrying out his deadly vow. Edward J. Dent, the great British operatic scholar, has called this "perhaps the most beautiful ensemble ever composed for the stage."

Its admirable qualities notwithstanding, *Idomeneo* languished for nearly two centuries in near-total obscurity. It was revived privately in Vienna in 1786 and during the nineteenth century

---

*Mozart had a remarkable ability to write for the voice. Richard Tucker, the American tenor, once told the author that singing Mozart was "like honey to the throat."

received an occasional performance, but only in Germany. Not until the early twentieth century did it reach Great Britain, in the form of a production by the Glasgow Garden Opera Society, composed mainly of amateurs. In 1951 the Glyndebourne Opera gave it its first professional performance in England, and several recordings were made after the advent of the long-playing era. It has finally become part of the repertory of both the Metropolitan Opera and the New York City Opera; probably it was the Met's performance of 1982, with Luciano Pavarotti in the title role, that made most Americans familiar with it.

Idomeneo may never become a genuinely popular opera in the sense of *Don Giovanni* or *The Magic Flute*. But its beautiful score retains a special appeal for musical connoisseurs, and it certainly demonstrates that when Mozart left Salzburg in 1781 to take up permanent residence in Vienna he already was a composer of undoubted genius.

Mozart in Vienna

"Just to be in Vienna is in itself entertainment enough."

—Mozart, letter to his father,
May 6, 1781

The Vienna in which Mozart settled was a city of around 200,000, the political capital of the Holy Roman Empire and the musical capital of the world. It has lost both of these distinctions, though the second far outlasted the first.

Even in Mozart's time the city's political heyday was almost over; the Holy Roman Empire, which, as Voltaire observed, was "neither holy, nor Roman nor an Empire," was on its last legs. In 1756, the year of Wolfgang's birth, it still encompassed Austria, Hungary, Bohemia, and various segments, some quite small, of Italy, Germany, and the Netherlands. But large parts of it had already broken away, and cracks were developing elsewhere.

The Austrian monarch in Mozart's early years was Maria Theresa, one of the most remarkable, though not amiable, women in European history. After the death of her husband, Francis I, in 1765, she decided to share the throne with her son Joseph II, but she never let go of the reins of power until her death at the age of sixty-three in 1780. When Joseph II took over as Emperor he considerably liberalized the government, trying to institute a degree of intellectual enlightenment and political and religious reform. To his surprise, many of his subjects preferred the old ways. He was not overly blessed with either diplomatic finesse or military expertise. The arts flourished under his regime, but affairs of state prospered only fitfully. The Holy Roman Empire's slow decline ended with its formal dissolution in 1806 by Joseph's nephew, Francis II.

Musically, however, Vienna in Mozart's time was just reaching its zenith. Indeed, no other city has ever served as the home base of so many great composers—first Mozart and Haydn, then Beethoven and Schubert, and, at the nineteenth century's end, Brahms and Mahler. Of these, only Schubert was actually born in the city, but all found an ambience and an audience that provided them with artistic stimulation. Vienna in Mozart's day was a musical melting pot; the city literally stood at a crossroads, the meeting place for composers and influences from Austria, Germany, Bohemia, Hungary, and Italy. It probably was the most musically cosmopolitan city that ever existed.

This is not to say that every Viennese understood or even loved music, or that large numbers of the nobility were appreciative of what a Mozart or a Haydn had to offer. In 1768 Leopold Mozart observed:

The Viennese public in general has no love of anything serious or sensible; and their theaters furnish abundant proof that nothing but utter trash, such as dances, burlesques, harlequinades, ghost tricks and devil's antics will go over with them. You may see a splendid gentleman wearing an order on his breast, laugh till the tears run down his face and applaud with all his might at some piece of senseless buffoonery; while in a truly affecting scene, where the situation and action alike are irresistibly fine and moving, and where the dialogue is of the highest order, he will chatter so loudly with a lady that his more knowledgeable neighbors can scarcely hear a word of the play.

Nevertheless, Wolfgang's initial years as a Viennese were successful to the point of exhilaration. Emperor Joseph II who, among his other reforms, wanted to foster a species of opera closer to ordinary people, had established in 1778 a new national opera company to present comedies in German. This style of musical theater was called Singspiel, or "singplay." The main action was presented in spoken dialogue, with songs and ensembles interspersed to permit the characters to comment or expand melodiously on a given situation. Mozart was among the composers commissioned by Joseph II to write works for this theater, and he responded with the opera *Die Entführung aus dem Serail*, usually translated as *The Abduction from the Seraglio* and best known in English simply as *The Abduction*.

Despite a number of stylistic and dramatic flaws (to cite only one, Pasha Selim, a pivotal character, never gets to sing a note), *The Abduction* was a huge success. In fact, it became Mozart's first true popular hit, by far the most frequently performed of his stage works during his lifetime. Revivals kept popping up; it was given forty-two times in Vienna between 1782 and 1788 and was produced in many other cities, too. In that pre-copyright era, of course, Mozart received precious little in recompense besides the modest sum he was paid for composing it.

For his principal financial support in Vienna, Mozart relied less on his capacities as a composer than on his prowess as a pianist. He was heartily tired of existing as the musical servant of a nobleman, but he would have been glad to have been appointed as a court composer, a position in which he would have had to write music on order but which would have left him his personal independence and the right to regulate his own life. When no such appointment seemed likely, he began to harbor the idea of arranging a kind of consortium of aristocrats who would back him financially and for whom he would create music. His plan, which he first conceived of on a visit to Munich in 1777, was for a minimum of ten wealthy individuals each to pay him a ducat a month, which, with other contributions he hoped to obtain, would amount to about the equivalent of a good job at court.

Leopold scoffed at such schemes, but Wolfgang realized, almost intuitively, that, as the old feudal way of providing courtly entertainment receded, new and more popular methods had to be found of supporting music and musicians. Unfortunately for him, he was a decade or two ahead of his time; when Ludwig van Beethoven made his advent in Vienna a few years afterward it was possible, if difficult, for a great composer to support himself. For Mozart it was not.

Public concerts were late in making their way to Vienna. The first concert society, the Tonkünstler, was not established there until 1771, a scant ten years before Mozart's arrival.

Even as a performer, Mozart found it difficult to get started economically in Vienna. "Nothing is more disagreeable than to have to live in uncertainty," he wrote to his father after his arrival. He kept informing Leopold about his projects for obtaining subsidies or support from various members of the aristocracy to assure himself "a small permanent income," but none ever came to fruition.

To make money, Mozart took pupils; but he didn't enjoy teaching particularly and some of his students dropped out after several lessons. He played at court and at private engagements, but for such recitals the honorarium tended to be minimal. To put it in a word, he scrounged. In a letter to his sister, written in his first year in Vienna, he described his daily routine—up at six A.M., composing until nine, giving piano lessons from nine to one P.M., lunching at one or two preferably at some aristocratic home—which meant spending hours in small talk and perhaps playing the piano some—finally, devoting himself to composition in the evening, unless there was a concert which he felt obliged to attend. Sometimes, he observed, he composed until one A.M.

Although Mozart's life underwent many changes and his fortunes rose and fell during his ten years in Vienna, this, essentially, was the kind of routine he maintained almost to the end of his life. He made a number of trips to cities like Prague, Munich, Dresden, Berlin, and Frankfurt, often connected with productions of his operas, and there was one protracted visit, after his marriage, to his father in Salzburg, but his home always remained Vienna.

Unfortunately Vienna, for its part, only welcomed Mozart with, to use the Gilbertian phrase, modified rapture. As a pianist Wolfgang created a sensation that lasted for several seasons. But as a composer, although he attracted the admiration of discerning listeners like Joseph Haydn, he was far from being a universal favorite. Rivals such as Karl Ditters von Dittersdorf, Leopold Anton Kozeluch, and Johann Baptist Wanhal, relatively lightweight composers whose music survives today only fitfully, were far more successful with the Viennese public. Many a Viennese musician achieved financial stability and security while Mozart struggled for a livelihood. Had he lasted a few years longer his situation might have changed, for fame came with an onrush after his death, but in his own day the musical public was curiously lukewarm to the greatest genius in its midst.

Mozart's success as a pianist entailed a great deal of extra-musical labor on his part. This was long before the era of agents, managers, concert circuits, organized tours, and the like; for the most part it was up to the performer himself to arrange for dates, hire halls, engage orchestral musicians, find subscribers, and sell tickets—all in addition to composing the music that was to be played!

However, a few individuals were attempting to set themselves up as what we should now call impresarios, and Mozart became associated with Jacob Philipp Martin, who organized a series of summer subscription concerts in Vienna's Augarten, a public garden in the suburb of Leopoldstadt, and other open spaces. Music by Mozart and others was on the programs, and Wolfgang set about selling subscriptions to his aristocratic friends and patrons. One of the concerts included his three-movement Symphony No. 34 in C, K. 338, and his Concerto for Two Pianos, K. 365, in which he and a pupil, Josephine Aurnhammer, played the solo parts. It went off, he reported to Leopold, "fairly well." Martin was so grateful to Mozart for his part in the garden concerts that he treated him to a fancy luncheon in the Augarten.

Wolfgang himself staged a series of three subscription concerts on successive Wednesdays at an establishment known as Trattner's Hall in March of 1784. "As you may imagine, I must play some new works, and therefore I must compose," he wrote to his father. He sent Leopold a list of 174 subscribers, consisting largely of counts and countesses, princes and princesses, barons and baronesses, and other persons of rank. Altogether, he told Leopold, he was scheduled for twenty-two performances, both private and public, over a five-week period. "With this, I can hardly get out of practice," he added jokingly. On many occasions Mozart had his own piano transported to the sites of his concerts. He also gave regular Sunday morning performances at his home, for which he charged admission.

The form that Mozart made peculiarly his own in Vienna was the piano concerto. The classical concerto hardly existed before him, but the combination of a solo instrument (often played by himself) with a full orchestra seemed particularly congenial to his musical mind. It enabled him to combine the lyricism of a solo instrumental voice with the broad range of development offered by a symphonic ensemble. Few songs or operatic arias, even by Mozart himself, are more touched with beauty or deeper in feeling than the slow movements of his greatest concertos. Nor was he limited to the piano, for he composed concertos for many instruments, including the flute, oboe, clarinet, bassoon, and horn.

The piano concertos, of course, also enabled him to display his own virtuosic abilities, although virtuosity for its own sake never much appealed to him. "I am no great lover of difficulties," he remarked, adding that "real playing" consisted of playing difficult passages in such a way that listeners were unaware of their difficulty. He derided pianists who grimaced and went through physical contortions at the keyboard, and he despised superficiality. Listening to one of his own concertos played at sight by Abbé Georg Joseph Vogler (later the hero of a famous poem by Robert Browning), Mozart told his father: "That kind of sight-reading and shitting are exactly the same to me. . . . It is much easier to play a thing quickly than slowly: in difficult passages you can leave out a few notes without anyone noticing it. But is that beautiful music?"

Mozart's skills as a pianist involved him in a head-to-head competition in 1781 with Muzio Clementi, an Italian-born virtuoso who had settled in England as a boy. The late eighteenth century loved such contests, and this was arranged by no less a personage than Joseph II himself. The emperor decided that Mozart had won because, he said, Wolfgang had played with both "art and taste" and Clementi with art alone. Clementi praised Mozart generously afterward, but Wolfgang, who was never noted for speaking well of his rivals, dismissed the Italian as a mere "*mechanicus*"—a technician.

Mozart's vogue as a concert performer in Vienna lasted only four or five years; his appearances became less frequent, possibly because their novelty appeal faded. From 1782 to 1786 he composed fifteen piano concertos, but by the age of thirty-two he had all but given up his career as a virtuoso; at least there is no record of further major concert appearances in Vienna. His last piano concerto, No. 27 in B-flat, a subdued autumnal masterpiece, was played at a concert given for a clarinetist friend of his.

Despite the indifference of so many Viennese, Mozart never thought seriously of leaving the city and relocating elsewhere. According to some accounts, he actually received offers to transfer his activities to Berlin, where King Frederick William of Prussia was an admirer of his music, or to London, where his friend Haydn had received such a warm welcome. Whenever such proposals were made, he rejected them. True, the Viennese musical public as a whole might prefer the works of a Salieri or a Kozeluch, but there were enough discerning connoisseurs to appreciate and applaud his own music—and that sufficed him. With all its superficiality and shallowness, late eighteenth-century Vienna was the center of the musical world, and that is where Mozart felt he belonged.

The Marriage of Wolfgang

"I, who from my youth have never been accustomed to look after my own things, linen, clothes and so forth, cannot think of anything I need more than a wife."

—Mozart, letter to his father,
December 15, 1781

Soon after he settled in Vienna Mozart got married and began raising a family. Women had always played a central role in his life—his mother, his sister, his cousin, his girlfriends in Salzburg and elsewhere. It was highly unlikely that as a leading light among the young musicians of Vienna he would long remain unattached.

The bride he chose—or, perhaps, the bride who chose him—was Constanze Weber, younger sister of Aloysia Weber, who had rejected him three and a half years before. Wolfgang and Constanze were married August 4, 1782, when he was twenty-six and she nineteen, after a courtship that had some curious aspects.

Chief among these was the role of Constanze's mother Maria Cäcilie, by all accounts a rather blowsy and boisterous woman who liked strong drink. Wolfgang originally had met the family in Mannheim, but now they had moved to Vienna. Maria Cäcilie's husband had recently died, and she supported herself and her three remaining unmarried daughters by taking in lodgers. What could be more natural than that Wolfgang, now at last on his own, should rent a room from her? At least so he wrote casually to Leopold: "Old Madame Weber has been good enough to take me into her house, where I have a nice room." Leopold was immediately suspicious; he had disliked the Weber clan ever since Wolfgang's first encounter with them years before in Mannheim, and now he apparently divined what Madame Weber had in mind for his son.

The musical world in Mozart's day was as gossipy as at any other time, and it was not very long before his relations with Constanze became a favorite topic among his Viennese ac-quaintances. A young rival composer, Peter von Winter, was especially assiduous in spreading stories; he called Constanze a *Luder* (slut) and said she was Mozart's mistress.*

Naturally, such tales reached Leopold back in Salzburg, and although Wolfgang kept denying any involvement with Constanze—"because I am living with them [the Webers], therefore I am going to marry the daughter," he wrote sarcastically—dissembling was not among his talents. Even though

---

*Ironically, after Mozart's death, this same Winter composed a sequel to *The Magic Flute* entitled *The Labyrinth*.

he moved to another lodging to quiet the rumors, the stories persisted. Indeed, Constanze was not the only girl to show an interest in him; his pupil Josephine Aurnhammer, he reported to his father, was "seriously enamored" of him. Then, with the candor that was not among his most endearing qualities, he added: "This young lady is a fright but plays enchantingly." The heavy-set, plain-looking Josephine eventually married a magistrate and became a highly successful concert pianist.

Mozart's involvement with Constanze Weber grew closer and closer until the girl's legal guardian, one Johann Thorwarth, a court theatrical official, appeared with a legal document and demanded that Wolfgang either agree to marry her within three years or pay her an annuity of 300 gulden ($1,500) a year. Then, according to the story Mozart told his incredulous father, Constanze immediately grabbed the document, tore it up, and said: "Dear Mozart, I need no written guarantee from you. I believe what you say."

Six months later Wolfgang and Constanze were married. Wolfgang went through the motions of asking for his father's permission, but he was determined to go ahead anyway. In actual fact, Leopold's formal permission arrived by mail the day after the wedding ceremony was performed. By now Leopold had given up on his son, not as a composer, certainly, but as a person whose destiny he could direct. Neither ever put his feeling into words, yet both were saddened by the breach that had opened between them. As artists they understood each other perfectly, but as human beings they occupied different worlds— father and son, teacher and pupil, conformist and rebel, realist and visionary. It was a rift that not even love could bridge.

What sort of person was Constanze Weber? Mozart, who nicknamed his bride "Stanzerl," described her this way: "She is not ugly, but at the same time far from beautiful. Her entire

Constanze Weber, who married Mozart after her sister Aloysia turned him down.

beauty consists of two little black eyes and a nice figure. She isn't witty, but has enough common sense to make her a good wife and mother. . . . She understands housekeeping and has the kindest heart in the world. I love her and she loves me. . . ."

Subsequent events would seem to verify Wolfgang's analysis

of his intended reasonably well, although the common sense and practicality he praises became more evident after Mozart's death than during their marriage which, after all, lasted only nine years. Constanze, who, it should be remembered, was only nineteen when they married, displayed a frivolous side that disturbed Wolfgang from time to time. Even before they were married he scolded her for allowing "a young man to measure the calves of your legs"; this event occurred during a game of "forfeits" as a penalty for giving an incorrect answer to a question. Mozart went on about it in considerable detail, to the point of suggesting that if Constanze ever found herself in a similar position again she should take the ribbon "and measure your calves yourself." On several occasions after their marriage he felt it necessary to urge her to show more propriety on her visits to Baden-bei-Wien, a nearby spa where she frequently went to take the curative baths.

But Constanze Mozart can hardly be said to have led a gay and carefree life. From June 1783, to July 1791, she bore six children. The Mozarts' first child, Raimund Leopold, died at the age of two months of "an intestinal cramp" while his parents were away on a visit to Salzburg. Their third, Johann Thomas Leopold, lived less than a month; their fourth, Theresia, six months; and their fifth, Anna Maria, only one hour. So there was a constant round of deaths, as well as births, in the Mozart household, each bringing with it its train of sorrow.

Mozart barely got to know either of his two surviving children, for when he died one was seven years old, the other less than six months. The older boy, Karl Thomas, born in 1784, in later life made several attempts at establishing a musical career, and once almost opened up a piano business in the Italian city of Livorno. But although he had received a basic musical education and inherited his father's piano, he never developed into a professional performer. He eventually wound up as a minor official on the staff of the viceroy of Naples in Milan. In 1842 he attended the unveiling of the Mozart monument in Salzburg and also participated in the centenary observances there in 1856. Karl Thomas Mozart died in 1858 at the age of seventy-four.

Franz Xaver Wolfgang Mozart came closer to inheriting his father's mantle. Indeed, Mozart's great rival Antonio Salieri, who was one of the boy's teachers, prophesied—quite inaccurately—that Franz Xaver would one day become as famous as his father. Actually, his musical skills were sufficient to justify a professional career, and he concertized extensively in Europe from Copenhagen to Kiev, calling himself—with the approval of his mother—Wolfgang Amadeus Mozart the Younger.

Franz Xaver spent many years in Lwow, Poland, where he composed, conducted, and served as a tutor in several aristocratic families. He maintained contact with his mother and elder brother, and also was present for the Salzburg dedication ceremonies of 1842. At a commemorative concert that highlighted the event he was the soloist in a performance of his father's D-minor Piano Concerto, K. 466. Franz Xaver Mozart died in Carlsbad in 1844, aged fifty-three. Perhaps the last word on "Wolfgang Amadeus Mozart the Younger" was best spoken by George Bernard Shaw in a letter he wrote to Ellen Terry, the actress, in 1897: "Do you remember—or did you ever hear of—the obscurity of Mozart's son? An amiable man, a clever musician, an excellent player; but hopelessly extinguished by his father's reputation. How could any man do what was expected from Mozart's son? Not Mozart himself even."

In recent years a number of pianists, notably the Canadian Julie Holtzman, have performed some of the younger Mozart's music, which is often of considerable charm. His works include two piano concertos, a string quartet, a piano trio, and many solo keyboard pieces and songs. One imagines that his father would have listened to them at least with affection.

Constanze's six pregnancies within nine years apparently had a debilitating effect upon her, for she made repeated visits to the nearby spa at Baden, thus contributing further to the already burdensome expenses of the Mozart household. Mozart sincerely missed his wife during her stays at the spa and occasionally went to visit her there. Similarly his letters to her during his travels to give concerts or stage operas in other cities are full of endearments.

But despite his affection for his wife, his name was linked— sometimes by contemporaries, more often by later commentators—with other women. In fact Constanze herself, long after his death, told interviewers that she believed her husband had indulged occasionally in what she called "servant-girleries." No actual affairs with women have ever been documented, and it is possible that he never slept with any besides his wife during his short married life. Nevertheless, here are three of those for whom he displayed at least a passing show of affection:

Nancy Storace   According to musicologist Alfred Einstein, Storace was "the only woman of whom Constanze would really have had a right to be jealous." Wolfgang was partial to sopranos, and Storace, who lived from 1766 to 1817, was a fine one. An Englishwoman, resident in Vienna, she created the role of Susanna in *The Marriage of Figaro*. Mozart admired her musically and personally. In 1784 she married John Abraham Fisher, an English violinist in Vienna, but soon separated from him and returned to London. She urged Mozart to come to England, and for some time maintained a correspondence with him, but the letters have been lost.

Henriette Baranius   Another soprano, a young singer at the opera in Berlin, Baranius reportedly was a favorite of the king of Prussia, Frederick William. Mozart heard her sing the role of Blondchen in *The Abduction from the Seraglio* on a visit to Berlin in 1790, and after the performance she asked him to give her further coaching in the part. Not unnaturally, rumors spread that their sessions together extended beyond musical matters.

Magdalena Hofdemel   This is the most curious of all of Mozart's supposed love affairs. Magdalena, the attractive young wife of Wolfgang's Masonic lodge brother Franz Hofdemel, was not a singer but a pianist, and one of Mozart's last keyboard pupils. A few days after Mozart's death, Magdalena, who was pregnant, was viciously attacked with a razor by her husband, who then committed suicide. Though badly slashed, she survived and five months later bore her child. Gossip spread in Vienna that she had been Mozart's mistress, that the child was really his, and that her husband attacked her in a fit of jealousy during a quarrel following Mozart's funeral. Among those giving some credence to the tale was Ludwig van Beethoven, who once resisted playing the piano in the presence of Magdalena because "too great an intimacy had existed between her and Mozart."

It is impossible to say whether Constanze believed such tales, any more than it is to determine how much stock Mozart put in stories that may have reached him about his wife's alleged indiscretions. Certainly the society in which both lived was profligate enough, with temptations especially prevalent in the musical-theatrical world. But on the actual evidence—as distinguished from the allegations—of infidelity for both, the verdict must be, at the very least, that nothing has been proven.

What sort of a musician was Constanze Mozart? By Mozartean standards, of course, hardly a notable one, yet she was not without qualifications. She had been raised in a musical household, and two of her sisters, Josepha and Aloysia, became successful professional singers. Constanze herself could play the piano, had a pleasing voice, and was skilled enough a performer to manage the difficult soprano part of Wolfgang's Mass in C minor, K. 427, in a performance at Salzburg. More than any of Mozart's other compositions, this work is hers, for Wolfgang had designed it as a thanksgiving mass in gratitude for their marriage. He never completed it, but even as it stands, with several missing movements, it is a powerful piece.

A curious change came over Constanze following Mozart's death in 1791. As indifferent as she had been as a wife, she turned into a perfect widow. During his lifetime she had never displayed much ability, or even interest, in managing the family's obligations and affairs. Mozart's death devastated her at first, but she determinedly pulled herself together to try to maintain herself financially and provide for the care and education of her two small sons. To raise money, she put on concerts of Mozart's music in several cities, appearing herself as a singer along with her sister Aloysia. She even got Beethoven to appear at one of them, playing a Mozart piano concerto. She also resorted to the Weber family's favorite method of support, renting rooms in her Vienna home. In 1797 one of her lodgers was Georg Nikolaus von Nissen, an official in the Danish Embassy. They became lovers and after the passage of twelve years—no one knows why it took so long—they were married.

Although Constanze was relatively uneducated and certainly no intellectual—her spelling and grammar, as displayed in her letters, were mediocre—she succeeded in attracting a cultivated and accomplished second husband, for Nissen, one year her senior, was not only a Danish State Councillor but a man of literary as well as musical interests. He was an ardent admirer of Mozart's music, and the circumstance that Constanze was the great composer's widow may indeed have enhanced her attractiveness to him. Not only did he see to her needs, he also took care of her two sons, who grew up regarding him with great warmth as the only father they ever really knew.

Whether because her pregnancies had ceased or her material well-being had undergone a change for the better, Constanze's health now suddenly improved. So, astonishingly, did her managerial skills and business abilities. With Nissen by her side, and the assistance of Abbé Maximilian Stadler, an old friend of the Mozarts who was an able musical scholar, she began organizing and cataloguing the manuscripts left by Wolfgang.

How can one explain Constanze's transformation from the rather empty-headed "dearest, most-beloved little Wife of My Heart" to whom Mozart addressed his ardent letters, into the shrewd, practical businesswoman who corresponded (with the guidance of Nissen, it is true) with publishers and editors about detailed musical and fiscal matters? The change may have simply reflected a difference of age—nineteen when she married Mozart, thirty-four when she took up with Nissen (forty-five when they finally married). Her rather precarious existence with Mozart may have tempered her. Or perhaps the difference was Nissen himself—far more practical, steady, and reliable than Mozart had ever been. Not for the first time in history, Constanze Mozart had demonstrated the difficulties a spouse finds in living happily with a genius. Now, with a sound, bourgeois, phlegmatic husband, she found at last contentment in marriage.

Nissen retired from the Danish government service in 1820, just as he was reaching sixty. He and Constanze settled in Salzburg where, among other attractions, he could work on a biography of Mozart, which was published in 1828, two years after its author died.

Constanze's last years, then, were spent in Mozart's birthplace. She had been widowed for the second time, but Nissen left her in sound financial shape. By now Mozart's fame was universal, and she was kept busy writing to correspondents and receiving travelers, some from abroad, who came with countless questions about her celebrated first husband.

Salzburg, indeed, in her time became a city of Mozartean ghosts, which, in a way, it has remained ever since. Constanze Mozart took into her house two of her sisters, Aloysia, Wolfgang's old flame who now was a widow herself, and Sophie, the youngest of the Weber girls, who had been a particular favorite of Mozart and who had helped nurse him through his last illness. Aloysia remained only briefly; Sophie stayed much longer. Mozart's son Franz Xaver Wolfgang was a frequent visitor to his mother in Salzburg.

And there also lived in Salzburg, after moving from the nearby town of St. Gilgen, Mozart's sister Nannerl. She had never much liked Constanze when she was married to her brother and saw no reason to change her opinion now that they both were old women who were neighbors. Constanze outlived Nannerl by a dozen years, dying at the age of seventy-nine in 1842, just a few months before the town of Salzburg dedicated the statue it erected to her husband after he had been dead for fifty years.

The Fiscal Mozart

"Flattering words, praise, and shouts of 'bravissimo' pay neither postmasters nor landlords."

—Leopold Mozart, letter to his son,
October 15, 1777

Among the most baffling aspects of Mozart's life is his seeming inability to make money. True, there were circumstances over which he had no control—accidents of timing, his wife's health needs (whether real or imaginary), even his premature death. But the impression remains that above all he simply lacked the gift of knowing how to turn his talents into hard cash. He may, indeed, have been so eager and prompt to provide a desired musical product that patrons shrewdly realized they could get what they wanted from him without paying very much for it. His genius was so bountiful that taking advantage of it was no problem.

His lack of the Midas touch manifested itself early, in his days as a child prodigy. Leopold Mozart had taken Wolfgang and Nannerl on their extended European tour in the hope of not only achieving fame but of reaping monetary benefits. However, the Mozarts came home not with hard cash but with a collection of gifts—snuffboxes, watches, pens, writing cases, fruit knives, shoe-buckles, toothpick cases, necklaces, earrings, medallions, and other portable objects. Leopold sold most of these after their return, so that he made a profit from the journey; nevertheless he found the aristocracy less generous in their recompense than he had hoped. "If kisses had been *louis d'or* we should have been quite content," he wrote unhappily to his Salzburg friend Lorenz Hagenauer after one particularly frustrating stop.

Wolfgang himself found much the same situation fifteen years later when he traveled with his mother on their ill-fated journey to Paris. During their long stopover in Mannheim he wrote to Leopold: "What one needs on a journey is money, and let me tell you, so far I have five watches. So I'm seriously thinking of having an extra watch pocket sewn on each leg of my trousers so I can wear two watches and when I visit an aristocrat he won't get the idea of giving me another one."

In Paris the joke turned serious because Wolfgang actually began running short of funds. Parisian impresarios and officials, sensing he had no head for money, took advantage of him and made promises they had no intention of keeping. Jean Le Gros, director of the Concerts Spirituels, kept commissioning works from him, and then either not playing them or not paying Mozart if he did. Wolfgang had to borrow money from his Parisian host Baron Grimm. He even pawned his mother's watch after she died—an action he didn't confess to Leopold until the latter wormed it out of him.

When Wolfgang returned to Salzburg and settled there in

his early twenties he could count on a steady if not lavish income in the service of Archbishop Colloredo. Together he and his father earned a combined salary of 1,000 gulden (nearly $5,000) a year, with Leopold receiving about three-fifths of this amount, Wolfgang two-fifths. In addition, of course, there was additional income to be obtained through teaching, and from commissions from such works as the opera *Idomeneo*. All through his life Mozart's problem was not that he didn't earn money, but that his expenses somehow always managed to exceed his income.

When Mozart threw over Salzburg and went to live on his own in Vienna he told his father that he expected to double his earnings in the Hapsburg capital. Indeed, for several years he did even better than that, for his scheme of organizing subscription concerts at which he appeared both as composer and pianist initially won an enthusiastic reception from aristocratic Viennese concertgoers.

Even the skeptical Leopold was impressed. In 1785, when Wolfgang was at his peak as a pianist-composer, his father paid him an extended visit in Vienna and reported that one concert had brought in 559 gulden—over $2,700. Leopold wrote to Nannerl that he calculated that Wolfgang ought to have about 2,000 gulden in the bank "if he has no debts to pay," which, as always with Mozart, was a very big if indeed.

While it is hard to judge today what such figures actually meant, there is no doubt that they represented far more in purchasing power in the late eighteenth century than they would now. Prices were modest. In 1786 one could enjoy for 31 kreuzer (half a gulden, or about $2.50) an excellent meal consisting of soup, two meat courses, vegetables, bread, and a quarter liter of wine. The standard fee for a composer to write an opera was 450 gulden, over $2,000, which was approximately the equivalent of Mozart's annual rent in the 1780s. We have records of the fees Mozart received for several of his operas—426 gulden for *The Abduction from the Seraglio*, 450 florins (the florin was worth less than the gulden) for *The Marriage of Figaro*. For *Don Giovanni*, which was commissioned by Prague, he received only 100 ducats (about $1,250), but its first performance in Vienna brought him nearly twice that amount as an additional honorarium.

Three concerts presented by Mozart every year during the Lenten season from 1784 to 1786 brought in 1,500 gulden annually, although there were, of course, considerable expenses attached to them, including hiring an orchestra. During Mozart's most productive years his annual income may have reached 10,000 gulden, or nearly $50,000, by eighteenth-century Viennese standards a handsome sum indeed.

All sorts of fantastic theories have been advanced to explain why Mozart couldn't make do on so substantial an income, including allegations that he was given to drink and to gambling for high stakes. But no real evidence has been adduced to support either theory. Nor can it be said that he was ignorant of the importance of money; from his early childhood it had been one of the principal topics of conversation in the Mozart household. In 1784, two years after his marriage, he attempted to keep a personal account book of his income and expenditures, jotting down such items as his expenditures of 1 kreuzer for flowers and 34 kreuzer for his pet starling. The record book only lasted for one year, after which he turned it over to Constanze, who couldn't be bothered keeping it up.

During the days of their relative affluence neither Mozart nor his wife was much given to economizing or saving. Constanze spent a good deal of money on her therapeutic trips to Baden, a resort both expensive and fashionable. Wolfgang traveled in style when he was away from Vienna, owned a horse on which he went riding regularly, and indulged in such other luxuries as having a *friseur* call practically every day at his home to dress his hair. The Mozarts also lived in high-rental quarters, some of which they couldn't really afford. They changed their dwelling places frequently in response to the ups and downs of their income, even moving outside of the city proper at one point. In 1787 Leopold observed in a letter to Nannerl: "Your brother is now living in the Landstrasse No. 224. He does not say why he has moved. Not a word. But unfortunately I can guess the reason." Mozart's yearly rent in the Landstrasse was only fifty gulden— far less than he had been accustomed to paying previously.

Mozart's financial situation deteriorated badly from 1786 on—that is, during the last five years of his life. He was no longer in demand as a pianist and his concert appearances dropped off sharply. Not only had the Viennese public, never very faithful or dependable, grown jaded; it's also possible that Wolfgang himself, then immersed in writing some of his most deeply felt and searching music, simply withdrew more and more into his inward artistic and personal struggles.

Whatever the reasons, he now needed money as never before. He had begun borrowing as early as 1783, perhaps going to usurers (though there is no actual record of this). But now he turned repeatedly to his friends, writing imploring letters asking for loans, some petty, some quite substantial. The recipients, particularly Michael Puchberg, a generous Masonic lodge brother, usually came through with the desired amount. They also kept his letters, presumably for their records. Puchberg, an attorney who had turned merchant and married a wealthy woman, usually jotted down the amount he had sent in a margin of the letter itself. Virtually all of the money was eventually repaid, either by Mozart himself or by his widow in the months after his death.*

---

*Puchberg also received by way of recompense a musical masterpiece, for Mozart dedicated to him his Divertimento in E-flat for String Trio, K. 563, which despite its casual-sounding title is one of his longest and most beautiful chamber compositions.

Mozart's letters to Puchberg must have been galling to write and cost him a tremendous price in lost pride. One can sense his feeling of humiliation as well as desperation even at an interval of 200 years: "Dearest, most beloved Friend. . . . Good God! I would not wish my worst enemy to be in my position today. And if you, my best friend and brother, abandon me, we are both lost, my miserable, innocent self and my poor sick wife and child. . . . I am coming to you not with thanks but with further begging. Instead of paying what I owe I am asking for more money! . . . Everything depends, my only friend, upon whether you can and will lend me another 500 gulden. Until I straighten out my affairs, I undertake to pay back ten gulden a month. . . ."

This is only one of a dozen letters Mozart sent to Puchberg within a single year, 1789, and he was borrowing from others at the same time. Yet very little of his straitened circumstances show in the letters he wrote almost simultaneously to his wife during her stays at the spa; these were unfailingly cheerful, optimistic, and tender. Mozart usually managed to put up a good front; a Viennese acquaintance named Josef Deiner, who worked at a neighborhood tavern, told in later years of finding Mozart and his wife dancing at their home with Wolfgang half-jokingly remarking that they were doing so to keep warm since they were out of firewood.

The closest that Mozart came to securing a steady income was in December of 1787 when Emperor Joseph II appointed him court chamber-composer, following the death of Christoph Willibald Gluck at the age of seventy-three. Gluck had received a stipend of 2,000 gulden in the position, but Joseph, who ran an economical court, reduced it to 800 (or about $4,000) for Mozart. After his death, Constanze was accorded one-third this amount as an annual pension.

Mozart's court salary contrasts sharply with the rewards

given other leading musicians in Vienna. When his successor as chamber composer, Leopold Anton Kozeluch, was appointed, the salary was immediately restored to 2,000 gulden. Antonio Salieri became a wealthy man as court Kapellmeister. Domenico Cimarosa, the Italian composer of *Il Matrimonio segreto*, who was named by Emperor Leopold II to succeed Salieri in 1791, was paid a salary of 12,000 florins or around $30,000. Mozart never saw money of that kind at the imperial court.

It is just possible that his situation might have improved if he had lived a few years longer. His opera *The Magic Flute*, which was premiered September 30, 1791, not at the court theater but at the popular Theater auf der Wieden, a 1,000-seat auditorium in the outskirts, was a tremendous success and was taken up enthusiastically by theaters throughout Europe. It is not known how much the producer (and librettist) of *The Magic Flute*, Emanuel Schikaneder, paid Mozart to write it, but the proceeds were enormous and presumably the composer would have shared in some of them.

Strangely, evidence of the tangled finances of Wolfgang Amadeus Mozart continues to crop up even in modern times. In 1964 a golden, diamond-studded pocketwatch, once given him by Empress Maria Theresa, was found after being missing for years. It had been hidden with other Austrian national treasures during World War II in a salt mine at Hallein, and after the war disappeared, having presumably been stolen. But an individual—who has never been identified—walked into the Mozarteum in Salzburg with it and turned it over. The Mozarteum promptly put it on exhibition.

In 1970 one of Mozart's begging letters was put up for sale by an auction house at Cologne. This was addressed in 1789 to Franz Hofdemel and asked for a loan of 100 gulden to tide Mozart over for a few weeks until his quarterly court salary payment arrived. Hofdemel, who was about to become a lodge brother of Mozart's, sent the money, equivalent to around $500, forthwith.

At the auction, Mozart's letter to Hofdemel fetched 21,000 deutsche mark, or $5,738—a sum that surely would have astonished the impoverished composer two centuries before.

Mozart and Haydn

*"I send my six sons to you, most celebrated and dear
friend. . . . Please receive them kindly, and be to them
a father, guide and friend."*

—Mozart, from his dedication
of a set of six string quartets
to Joseph Haydn, September 1, 1785

Musical history is not exactly replete with stories of
close friendships between composers. Artistic differences, conflicting ambitions, and competitive pressures tend to
promote rivalry rather than concord. Certainly musical Vienna
in Mozart's day was a nest of intrigue, contention, and factionalism, with musicians from all over middle Europe, not to mention Italy, vying for commissions, preferment, and royal favor.
Against this background the friendship between Mozart and

Franz Joseph Haydn, which began in 1781 and lasted until Wolfgang's death ten years later, assumes a memorable, almost a mythic, quality, both artistically and personally. Haydn, born in 1732, was twenty-three years older than Mozart, and he outlived him by eighteen years, dying in 1809. Haydn's life span was more than double that of Mozart; chronologically, at least, he belonged to an earlier generation.

Yet a close affinity sprang up between them almost from their first meeting in Vienna. Mozart, who could be candid to the point of cruelty in his appraisal of other musicians, was quick and open in his affirmation of Haydn's superiority over the other composers of the time, and Haydn, one of the few musicians perceptive enough to divine the extent of Mozart's talents, was equally prompt and cordial in his recognition. It was a case, simply, of two geniuses embracing each other with generosity, almost with reverence.

Actually, Mozart had every reason to know of Haydn's music long before he met him. The Haydn family came from Rohrau, near the Danube in lower Austria. Authorities differ as to whether they originally were of Hungarian or Croatian ancestry. Joseph and his younger brother Michael became musicians and went to Vienna as boys for education and training. Neither remained there, however, for Joseph wound up as a Kapellmeister at the estate of Prince Paul Anton Esterházy at Eisenstadt in Hungary, while Michael settled in Salzburg in 1762 as a musician at the court of Prince-Archbishop Sigismund Schrattenbach and stayed on under the regime of Hieronymus Colloredo.

Thus the young Mozart found Michael Haydn one of the fixtures of his life at Salzburg, as a performer (he played the violin and organ and also conducted), as a composer, and to a degree as a friend. While not nearly a composer of the quality of his elder brother, Michael Haydn wrote prolifically, producing some 400 choral compositions, 60 symphonies, several operas, and a great variety of songs and instrumental pieces. Michael was something of a tippler and, according to Leopold Mozart, on one occasion showed up drunk at a service for which he was organist and played "so badly that we all were horrified."

Nevertheless, Wolfgang appears to have cherished a liking for him and for his music. When Haydn fell temporarily ill (or was otherwise incapacitated) Mozart obligingly wrote some music for him, including two duets for violin and viola (K. 423 and 424) and the introduction for a symphony (K. 444). Unlike Wolfgang, Michael Haydn loved Salzburg, resisting offers of more lucrative positions elsewhere and dying there in 1806.

Through Michael, of course, Mozart would have had plenty of opportunity to become acquainted with the music of Joseph Haydn. Actually he would have been well aware of this music in any case, for the senior Haydn, though his greatest masterpieces still lay in the future, was already one of Europe's best-known musicians.

By the time Joseph Haydn met Mozart during a visit to Vienna as part of the Esterházy entourage he was already the composer of more than seventy symphonies and forty string quartets. Throughout his long life his artistry grew at a deliberate pace rather than flowering suddenly; undoubtedly it was to his advantage to be able to develop and experiment musically at the remote Esterházy estate rather than to be caught up in the pressures of the Viennese musical rat race.

The friendship between the older composer and the younger deepened during a prolonged stay that Haydn made in Vienna with Prince Nicholas Esterházy in the winter of 1784–85. Haydn put on a number of musical evenings at the Esterházy palace in Vienna, and invited Mozart to participate in these. Wolfgang, then at his peak as a clavier player and a composer of concertos,

Barbara Krafft's oil painting of Mozart at twenty-five. Though done after his death, it was considered an excellent likeness by those who knew him.

admired Haydn's string quartets and conceived the idea of writing a set of six which he dedicated to the older man. In a rather flowery inscription Mozart described these works as "six sons" which he hoped would "one day prove a source of consolation" to himself and which in the meantime he was entrusting "to the protection and guidance of a man who is very celebrated and who also happens to be his best friend."

Haydn accepted the dedication warmly. While in Vienna he frequently visited Mozart's dwelling, joining him in impromptu chamber music performances. We even know the makeup of the string quartet that performed the music of Haydn, Mozart, and others at these soirées—Haydn, first violinist; the composer Karl Ditters von Dittersdorf, second violinist; Mozart, violist; and the composer Johann Baptist Wanhal, cellist. Mozart said he preferred to play the viola rather than the violin in a quartet because it enabled him to sit "in the middle" and hear the music all around him. Curiously, Johann Sebastian Bach had made the same observation fifty years before.

Among the most interested onlookers at—and probably participants in—these musical soirées was Leopold Mozart, who had come to visit his son in Vienna early in 1785. After a performance at Mozart's home Haydn turned to Leopold and said: "I tell you before God, as an honest man, that your son is the greatest composer I know, either personally or by name. He has taste and moreover the greatest science in composition."

These were words which Leopold Mozart had been waiting to hear someone speak for half his life, and coming as they did from the most celebrated and revered composer in Europe they must have gladdened his soul and made his years of hope, labor, and sacrifice seem worthwhile. Leopold reported Haydn's remark proudly in a letter he wrote to Nannerl; he also added that he had heard a "glorious concerto" by Wolfgang (No. 17

in G, K. 453) in which the interplay of instruments was so beautiful "that tears came to my eyes for sheer delight." The emperor had attended the performance and cried out "Bravo, Mozart!" waving his hat as he did so. It had been a good week for Leopold Mozart.

The interrelation between Mozart and Haydn was musical as well as personal. Mozart's quartets gained in structural strength and tightness from his exposure to Haydn's. Haydn learned a great deal from Mozart's masterly handling of wind instruments. Each deepened the other's art.

Haydn confided to Mozart that he had been invited to London by the British impresario Johann Peter Salomon. Mozart, who later was to receive a similar offer, tried to talk the older man out of going. The crossing was arduous, he said, and the English language difficult. "My language is understood all over the world," Haydn replied. The outcome of the trip proved him right, for the twelve symphonies he wrote for Salomon in London were enormously successful and have remained his most popular symphonies to this day.

Haydn must have realized that Mozart was having a difficult time of it financially, for he never missed an opportunity to praise his work or to help obtain a commission for him. In 1787, for example, he was asked to compose an opera for Prague. In the course of declining, on the grounds that he had a prior obligation to his own theater at Esterháza, he urged the producers to contact Mozart, whose *Don Giovanni* had recently been premiered in Prague.

"It is hardly possible for anyone to stand beside the great Mozart," he wrote. "If I could impress upon the soul of every music-lover, especially those in high places, the deep musical understanding and keen feeling which I myself have for Mozart's inimitable works, the nations would compete for such a jewel within their borders. Prague should hold on to this precious man tightly, but pay him well, too. . . . It enrages me to think that the unique Mozart has not yet been engaged by an Imperial or royal court!"

When Haydn left for England in December 1790, he spent his last day in Vienna in the company of Mozart. They parted in tears. Mozart said: "I fear, father, that this will be our last farewell"—though he appears to have been concerned about the health of Haydn, who was near sixty, rather than his own.

Haydn was still in London when Mozart died a year later. He wrote to Michael Puchberg in Vienna that he was "quite beside myself over his death" and that he—a deeply religious man—could hardly believe that "Providence should so quickly have called away an irreplaceable man into the next world." He asked Puchberg to send him a list of Mozart's works that might be available for publication in England.

He also wrote to Constanze telling her that if he could find a publisher he would forward all the proceeds to her, and offering to teach her son Karl Thomas composition when he came of age. When his own English publisher expressed an interest in acquiring a collection of Mozart pieces Haydn said: "Buy it by all means. He was truly a great musician. Friends flatter me by saying that I possess some genius, but he stood far above me."

Thus did one great musician take his leave of another. Haydn died in 1809; at his funeral the music performed was Mozart's Requiem.*

---

*It also was performed following Beethoven's funeral in 1827.

Mozart and England

"I have heard of England's victories and am greatly delighted, for you know that I am a dyed-in-the-wool Englishman."

—Mozart, letter to his father,
October 19, 1782 (following battles by the British fleet
off Gibraltar and Trincomalee, India)

Once when Leopold Mozart was busy proferring advice to his son, then en route to Paris, he offered this apothegm: "Always be natural with people of high rank; with everybody else behave like an Englishman." In the same letter he explains that he means it is best to maintain a discreet reserve with most people—*"de la politesse et pas d'autre chose."*

Whether the advice was intended to be taken literally or not, there is no doubt that Leopold Mozart greatly admired the English in many ways, and that his son shared his feelings.

Although Wolfgang spent more than a year in England, he was only nine years old when he departed, so his impressions of the country and the people, while pleasant, can hardly have been decisive in forming his opinions.

Nevertheless, throughout his life he showed a predilection for English people and English ideas. As noted, one of his earliest friends was Thomas Linley, the English lad of thirteen he encountered in Florence on his first tour of Italy. When he settled in Vienna he once again found companionship among the British musicians who had migrated there.

Among these were Stephen and Nancy Storace, brother and sister, who had come to Vienna in 1784, the latter to sing, the former to play the violin and compose. Nancy was ten years younger than Mozart, Stephen, seven.

Both of the Storaces were highly gifted musicians, with Nancy developing into one of the most sought-after and highly paid sopranos of her time. She specialized in soubrette parts and was picked by Mozart to sing Susanna at the premiere of *The Marriage of Figaro*. Both Storaces were lively individuals and at the center of a little group of Britishers working in Vienna which also included Thomas Attwood, a twenty-year-old organist who took lessons from Mozart, and Michael Kelly, a Dublin-born tenor who also was in the first cast of *The Marriage of Figaro*, doubling in the parts of Basilio the music master and Don Curzio the stuttering notary.

Mozart spent much time in the company of this convivial group, and practiced his halting English on them. Sometimes he would even try to write in English. Attwood saved a note from him, written on a sheet of music: "This after noon I am not at home, therefore I pray you to come to morrow at three & a half. Mozart."

Most of the English group left Vienna to return home early in 1787 and, as they were traveling by way of Salzburg, Wolfgang urged them to stop off to visit his father and sister. While there Nancy gave a little concert for Archbishop Colloredo. Leopold gallantly played host to the group, although he was ailing—he died less than a month later. He wrote to Wolfgang that he had "galloped around the town with them" for the better part of a day showing them the sights. He also observed, almost enviously, that the English group was traveling with eight horses and a prodigious amount of baggage.

While all of his British friends remembered and talked about Mozart for years afterward, only Michael Kelly, the Irish tenor, wrote an extended memoir of him—one of the most revealing descriptions left behind by any of his contemporaries.

Kelly himself was a remarkable character. Born in 1762, and thus five years younger than Mozart, he also spelled his name O'Kelly and, in Italy, Occhelli. Mozart listed him in his catalogue as "Occhelly." Following a seven-year sojourn in Italy and Austria he returned to London, where he became active as a singer, composer, and musical manager. He also went into the wine business and opened a shop with a signboard inscribed MICHAEL KELLY, IMPORTER OF WINES AND COMPOSER OF MUSIC. This led Richard Brinsley Sheridan, the playwright, who knew that Kelly borrowed from Italian musical sources and also that he blended his wines, to say that the sign really should read COMPOSER OF WINES AND IMPORTER OF MUSIC.

Kelly's account of Mozart is contained in his *Reminiscences*, published in London in 1826. He tells of meeting Mozart at a private concert followed by a party, a meeting he calls "one of the greatest gratifications of my musical life." Then he goes on with both a personal and a musical description:

> He favored the company by performing fantasias and *capriccios* on the pianoforte. His feeling, the rapidity of his fingers, the great execution and strength of his

left hand, particularly, and the apparent inspiration of his modulations, astounded me. After this splendid performance we sat down to supper, and I had the pleasure to be placed at table between him and his wife, Madame Constance Weber, a German lady of whom he was passionately fond, and by whom he had three children. He conversed with me a good deal about Thomas Linley, the first Mrs. Sheridan's brother, with whom he was intimate at Florence, and spoke of him with great affection. He said that Linley was a true genius, and he felt that, had he lived, he would have been one of the greatest ornaments of the musical world. After supper the young scions of our host had a dance, and Mozart joined them. Madame Mozart told me, that great as his genius was, he was an enthusiast in dancing, and often said that his taste lay in that art, rather than in music.

He was a remarkable small man, very thin and pale, with a profusion of fine fair hair, of which he was rather vain. He gave me a cordial invitation to his house, of which I availed myself, and passed a great part of my time there. He always received me with kindness and hospitality. He was remarkably fond of punch, of which beverage I have seen him take copious draughts. He was also fond of billiards, and had an excellent billiard table in his house. Many and many a game have I played with him, but always came off second best. He gave Sunday concerts, which I always attended. He was kind-hearted, and always ready to oblige, but so very particular when he played that, if the slightest noise were made, he instantly left off. . . .

Encouraged by his flattering approbation, I attempted several little airs, which I showed him, and which he kindly approved of, so much indeed, that I determined to devote myself to the study of counterpoint and consulted with him, by whom I ought to be instructed. He said, "My good lad, you ask my advice and I will give it you candidly; had you studied composition when you were at Naples and when your mind was not devoted to other pursuits, you would have perhaps done wisely; but now that your profession of the stage must, and ought, to occupy all your attention, it would be an unwise measure to enter into a dry study. You may take my word for it, nature has made you a melodist, and you would only disturb and perplex yourself. Reflect, 'a little knowledge is a dangerous thing;' should there be errors in what you write, you will find hundreds of musicians, in all parts of the world, capable of correcting them, therefore do not disturb your natural gift."

"Melody is the essence of music," continued he; "I compare a good melodist to a fine racer, and counterpointists to hack post horses, therefore be advised, let well enough alone, and remember the old Italian proverb—'Chi sa più, meno sa'—'who knows most, knows least.' " The opinion of the great man made on me a lasting impression.

With so many English friends it was inevitable that the thought of a visit to London should enter Mozart's mind. He even began to practice the language against the eventuality that he might actually go. In 1787 he inscribed an English sentence in the album of a friend who collected aphorisms. It was marred by only one spelling error and a slight grammatical awkwardness: "Patience and tranquillity of mind contribute more to cure our distempers as the whole art of medecine [sic]." It is not known whether the sentiment is Mozart's own or a quotation. About this time he also began to acquire English-language books, several of which were listed in the inventory of his effects after his death. One, edited by Friedrich Wilhelm Streit and published in Germany in 1774, bore the curiously elaborate title: *An attempt to facilitate the learning of the English language by publishing a collection of some letters, anecdotes, remarks and verses, wrote [sic!] by several celebrated English authors.*

Under the prodding of the Storaces, Mozart actually suggested to Constanze that they undertake a voyage to England in 1786 and, had he been on better terms with his father, he might actually have done so. His problem then was that he had two small children, Karl Thomas and Johann Thomas Leopold (who subsequently died), whom he could hardly take along. So he wrote to Leopold proposing that he and his wife leave the babies with him in Salzburg. Leopold peremptorily rejected the suggestion, writing sarcastically to Nannerl: "Not at all a bad arrangement! They would go off and travel—might even die— or stay on in England—leaving me to run after them with the children. As for the payment he offers me to take care of the children and their nursemaid—*basta!* If he's interested he'll find my response instructive and to the point!" Wolfgang never mentioned the matter to his father again; if he had ever doubted the width of the chasm that separated them he now realized it fully.

Mozart's British friends continued to perform his music in London; publishers there brought out several of his works; his compositions were presented at outdoor festivals as well as in concert halls. The poet Leigh Hunt, born in 1784, said that he had his first exposure to Mozart's music as a child when he heard an open-air band at St. James Park play an arrangement of *"Non più andrai"* from *The Marriage of Figaro.*

But it must not be supposed that Mozart's music in any way swept through England after his death; in addition to the unavailability of so much of it, there also was plenty of competition. The British never lost their love for Handel; they developed a warm affection for Haydn; and they were carried away by the newly arrived music of Beethoven, who became the favorite composer of the Philharmonic Society, established in 1813. However, in 1829 it was the Philharmonic subscribers who raised the sum of sixty pounds to be conveyed to Nannerl Mozart by Vincent and Mary Novello. The house of Novello also published some of the music of both Mozart and Haydn.

Leigh Hunt was one of the earliest proselytizers for Mozart's music in London. Hunt, the author of such poems as "Jenny Kissed Me" and "Abou Ben Adhem," represents one of the earliest instances of that rare phenomenon—it flourishes more frequently in England than in America—the literary man with musical knowledge and taste. He printed a great deal of musical criticism in two journals he edited, the *Examiner* and the *Reflector*. Imprisoned for two years for publishing political criticisms of the prince regent, he wrote letters from his cell proposing that the Novellos publish a set of Mozart songs.

Hunt inculcated a love of Mozart among several of the rising generation of English Romantic poets, including John Keats and Percy Bysshe Shelley. Keats, indeed, mentioned Mozart in one of his earliest (and not, unfortunately, best) poems, the "Epistle to Charles Cowden Clarke":

> *But many days have passed since last my heart*
> *Was warm'd luxuriously by divine Mozart. . . .*

More memorable is Keats's description in a letter to a friend of the effect made upon him by an exotically beautiful woman he had met in October 1818: "She kept me awake one night, as a tune of Mozart's might do." William Makepeace Thackeray made a strikingly similar comparison in his *Sketches and Travels in London*, published in 1879: "When she comes into the room, it is like a beautiful air of Mozart breaking upon you."

It took about twenty years for Mozart's operas to reach London. *La Clemenza di Tito* arrived in 1806, *The Magic Flute* in 1812, *Così fan tutte* not until 1828 under the title of *Tit for Tat, or The Tables Turned*, with the music drastically rearranged. Performances were often slapdash. Thomas Love Peacock, another poet with musical inclinations, remarked that *The Marriage of Figaro* and *The Magic Flute* "both require a better and more numerous company than is ever assembled in this country." Of *The Magic Flute*, which was given in Italian, he observed: "*Il Flauto Magico* is a well-written libretto, but the subject is too mystical to be interesting, or even generally intelligible; and this is a great drawback on its theatrical popularity . . . though the music exhausts all the fascinations of both melody and harmony, and may be unhesitatingly cited as the absolute perfection of both. It requires more good singers. . . . We may therefore despair of ever hearing this opera performed as it ought to be."

The supreme success of Mozart's operas in England was *Don Giovanni*, which, with its demonic lover, spoke most clearly to the young romantics of England as well as to those of other lands. Its first London production at the King's Theater on April 12, 1817, made an extraordinary impact, setting off all sorts of imitations and parodies. According to a publication called *The Drama, or Theatrical Pocket Magazine* for November 1821, Mozart's opera "ran through the whole season with the greatest applause, proving the most profitable speculation that house had entered into for many a year. . . . Since then Don Juan has appeared upon the English stage in various forms from a serious opera to a ballet, pantomime and burlesque, and has played at every theater in the metropolis."

One of the earliest of these appearances was in a Drury Lane pantomime, which ended in the infernal regions with the Don showered by fire and surrounded by dancing devils. On other London stages the Don appeared in such guises as a horseman, a Harlequin, and a vampire. A parody called *Giovanni in London* by one W. T. Moncrieff was produced in 1820 in Bath, where it had an extended run, although one observer sourly remarked that its success depended mainly "on the merits of Madame Vestris' legs." In 1845 Edward Holmes, a friend of Keats and a member of his circle, published the first biography of Mozart in English, an excellent book that is still available in the Everyman's Library series.

Don Giovanni aside, performances of Mozart's operas gradually faded out; the age of Bellini and Donizetti and of the bel canto singers had arrived. Mozart suddenly seemed old-fashioned and a little precious. Although some of his instrumental music continued active, it too seemed to its nineteenth-century listeners to suffer alongside the more outspoken utterances of Beethoven and his successors. After 1850 Mozart was represented in English concert halls at best by a handful of symphonies and a piano concerto or two.

Professor Edward J. Dent summed up the course of Mozart's music in his classic work *Mozart's Operas*, published in 1913: "The nineteenth century began by adopting Mozart as the fashionable novelty; within a few generations it had established him as a classic, and it ended by relegating him for the most part to the schoolroom as a composer of sonatinas for little girls to practise."

Fortunately the twentieth century has seen a complete reversal of this attitude, with the British playing a leading role in the revival not only of Mozart's instrumental music but in the performance of his operas with authenticity and insight. Sir

Thomas Beecham, the conductor, had a good deal to do with that revival, but perhaps the most significant role was that played by the Glyndebourne Opera of John Christie, who in 1934 began giving, in an eight hundred-seat theater on his private estate, meticulously prepared and musically elegant performances of the major Mozart operas. Through recordings, released originally in the United States by RCA, the Glyndebourne Opera opened the eyes and ears of music lovers on both sides of the Atlantic to the long-hidden beauties of these masterpieces, so that today they are universally known and appreciated. Mozart's English friends have remained steadfast for two centuries.

The da Ponte Saga

*"Our poet here is now a certain Abbate Da Ponte.
. . . He has promised to write a new libretto for me.
But who knows whether he will?"*

—Mozart, letter to his father,
May 7, 1783

Although the name of Lorenzo da Ponte remains alive principally because he was Mozart's librettist, he himself was one of the most fascinating literary adventurers of his time. He cut a swath through the best societies of Vienna, London, and New York, hobnobbed with royalty, circulated among literary and musical lions, and finally wound up his career in the unlikely post of professor of Italian at Columbia University.

Da Ponte was born a Jew, one of several such with whom

Mozart was intimately associated during his life.* His real name was Emanuele Conegliano and he was born March 10, 1749 at Ceneda, a town near Venice which since 1918 has been known as Vittorio Veneto in commemoration of an Italian military victory over the Austrians. His father, a tanner by trade, was named Geremia, his mother Rachele. They had three sons, Emanuele, Baruch, and Anania, who seemed destined to live out their lives as inhabitants of the little town's ghetto. Their native tongue was a mixture of Hebrew and the local Venetian dialect.

Rachele died soon after the birth of her third son, and Geremia Conegliano, now forty years old, fell in love with a sixteen-year-old Christian girl. To facilitate his remarriage to her, Conegliano decided to undergo baptism and become a Catholic, putting his sons through the same rite. The bishop performing the ceremony in the Ceneda cathedral was Monsignor Lorenzo da Ponte, and, following the custom of the time, the four converts all adopted the last name of their sponsor, with the oldest boy taking his first name as well. Thus Geremia became Gaspare da Ponte, Emanuele became Lorenzo da Ponte, and his two younger brothers Girolamo and Luigi da Ponte. Geremia, incidentally, went on to have ten more children by his fecund second wife.

Young Lorenzo da Ponte, fourteen at the time of his baptism, was a sharp-witted boy who realized that his surest path to advancement in life was through an ecclesiastical education. So he entered the Ceneda Seminary, where he concentrated on Latin studies while also pursuing a newly developed taste for Italian classical literature. He emerged as a priest although, as he later wrote in an uncharacteristic outburst of candor, "this was completely contrary to my vocation and character."

*See following chapter.

Six months after being ordained he decided to move to Venice, then one of the most profligate cities in Europe—a condition greatly to his liking. Da Ponte, who was twenty-four years old, acquired a succession of mistresses in Venice, lost a good deal of money at the gambling tables, and found it prudent to skip town from time to time, sometimes for extended periods. During intervals of relative calm he managed to pursue a literary career of sorts.

After one particularly scabrous episode in which he was accused of "seducing a married woman and living with her outside the sacraments," Lorenzo shifted his operations to Vienna. It was a city in which most of the creative personalities were young people. Antonio Salieri, the official court composer who pretty much ran the musical establishment, was thirty-two, da Ponte was the same age, Mozart was twenty-six. Da Ponte succeeded in attaching himself to Joseph II's court as Imperial Poet, and started out by writing librettos for Salieri.

But his initial efforts were not particularly successful, so he was very much on the lookout for musical collaborators. He settled upon Mozart and Vicente Martin y Soler, a twenty-eight-year-old Spaniard who spent several productive years in Vienna before moving on to Saint Petersburg, where he died in 1796.*

For Mozart, finding a gifted librettist was vital. He is, after all, the only great composer equally at home in both opera and symphony. No one has ever surpassed his ability to create human characters in music, and few have taken as much care in selecting and working out the librettos of his stage pieces. He once told his father that he had "looked through at least a hundred libretti and more" without finding one to his satisfaction. He also laid down the dictum that "in opera the poetry must be the obedient

*Martin was the composer of the opera *Una cosa rara*, a theme from which is quoted by Mozart in the supper scene of *Don Giovanni*.

daughter of the music," adding: "The best thing of all is when a good composer, who understands the stage and is talented enough to make sound suggestions, meets an able poet."

Mozart insisted on playing a decisive part in shaping the dramatic concept of his operas and on giving the musical content the predominating role. He was always ready to do battle with a librettist who wasn't giving him what he wanted. Working on his opera *Idomeneo*, for which a libretto was written by Giambattista Varesco, court chaplain at Salzburg and a clumsy poet, Wolfgang, who was all of twenty-four years old, kept making changes and revisions to suit his own needs.

At one point he remarked to his father that he was reducing the length of an offstage declamation by a subterranean oracle, remarking, by way of comparison: "If the speech of the Ghost in *Hamlet* were not so long it would be far more effective." (He had just seen a performance of Shakespeare's play by a touring company in Salzburg.) With fine disdain he cut and trimmed the *Idomeneo* libretto, assuring his father that Varesco would surely not mind just so long as everything appeared as he had written it in the printed—as opposed to the sung—version of the text.

In da Ponte Mozart found a librettist he could work with on an equal footing, as one practiced professional to another. The two collaborators never became intimate friends, any more than W. S. Gilbert and Arthur Sullivan did, but they formed a remarkably successful and cohesive team, producing three masterful works, *The Marriage of Figaro, Don Giovanni*, and *Così fan tutte*.

Figaro, the first of the great triumvirate of Italian-language operas, was Mozart's idea. He seems to have selected the subject for two reasons, the first being the dramatic appeal and variety of its characters: an aristocratic couple in a state of marital tension; their shrewd and likable valet and maidservant, about to get married; an amorous youth; a drunken gardener; and a set of assorted court hangers-on. The second reason was more prosaic and practical: Mozart knew that the original French satire by Pierre-Augustin Caron de Beaumarchais had achieved notoriety throughout Europe and that, even shorn of its political implications, it was bound to attract attention and audiences. Besides, a highly successful operatic version of Beaumarchais's other Figaro play, *The Barber of Seville*, had already been made by the Italian composer Giovanni Paisiello.* Mozart was never one to ignore the potential box-office appeal of his operas.

The political background of *The Marriage of Figaro* almost prevented its production, but da Ponte, a skilled intriguer, succeeded in convincing Joseph II that all potentially offensive material had been removed, and also that Mozart had written some "remarkably beautiful music."

Da Ponte later overcame another attempt to wreck the opera. A court faction opposed to the production objected to the inclusion of the fandango scene in Act III, during which the wedding of Figaro and Susanna is celebrated by a dance. These opponents argued that Joseph II, in one of his austerity measures, had ordered that ballets be excluded from operas produced at court. Da Ponte and Mozart both contended that the scene was not a formal ballet but an episode integrated into the main action. To prove their point they had the idea of presenting the dance scene in total silence and without music at the dress rehearsal, which Joseph attended. When the emperor demanded to know what was going on, da Ponte explained the situation

---

*Paisiello's *Barber*, first produced in 1782, in Saint Petersburg, was one of the most popular operas of its day in Italy. It was totally eclipsed, however, when Gioacchino Rossini's opera on the same subject premiered in Rome in 1816.

bluntly, and the Emperor promptly ordered the scene restored —with music.

It never has been clear exactly who attempted to impede the production of *The Marriage of Figaro* or the motives behind the scheme, but intrigue was particularly rife in the Vienna of the classical era, and Mozart—always poor at such maneuvering —benefitted in practical as well as literary ways from his association with da Ponte.

Of course da Ponte had other collaborators besides Mozart. By the time he came to publish his *Memoirs* in New York, starting in 1823, Mozart's fame was assured, and the librettist filled his book with such self-congratulatory assertions as: "I can never remember without exultation and complacency that it was to my perseverance and firmness alone that Mozart and the world in great part owe the exquisite vocal compositions of that admirable genius."

A bit more historically accurate, perhaps, is his recollection of the pleasurable time he himself had working on the libretto of *Don Giovanni*:

> I sat down at my table and did not leave it for twelve hours at a stretch—a bottle of Tokay on my right, a box of Seville tobacco on my left, an inkwell in the middle. A beautiful girl of sixteen—I should have preferred to love her only as a daughter, but . . . !— was living in the house with her mother, the housekeeper, and came to my room whenever I rang a bell. To tell the truth, the bell rang rather frequently, especially whenever I felt my inspiration failing. . . .

Actually, da Ponte recounts with great pride, he was working on the librettos of two other operas at the same time, *Axur* for

Salieri and *L'arbore di Diana* for Martin y Soler. Martin was a particular favorite of da Ponte; as it turned out, the Spaniard's *Una cosa rara*, for which da Ponte also supplied the libretto, proved a far greater success in Vienna than *The Marriage of Figaro*.

Da Ponte remained in Vienna until the death of his patron, Joseph II, in 1790. After vainly trying to persuade Mozart to go with him to England, he bumped around Europe for nearly three years. During this period he renewed an old friendship with Giacomo Casanova, the almost legendary great lover, now employed in his declining years as librarian for Count Waldstein at the castle of Dux in Bohemia. Casanova, who is thought by some to have contributed several verses to da Ponte's libretto for *Don Giovanni*, advised his old friend to try his luck in London. Instead, da Ponte spent a good deal of time in Trieste. There, late in 1791, he learned of the death of Mozart, without any apparent show of emotion.

In Trieste, also, he decided to get married, a move that was somewhat surprising since he was, technically at least, still a Catholic priest, not to mention the possessor of a well-earned reputation as a philanderer. But such considerations never bothered da Ponte; as a matter of fact, the girl he married, Nancy Grahl, was Jewish, the daughter of John Grahl, a German-born merchant who had lived many years in England. Reports even circulated that they had been married according to the Jewish rite. Nancy was twenty years younger than da Ponte, and endowed with spirit, energy, and intelligence. When da Ponte took her to meet Casanova he introduced her as his mistress rather than his bride, apparently being ashamed to admit to his licentious friend that he had finally broken down and entered upon matrimony. Surprisingly, Lorenzo's marriage to Nancy turned out to be a love match which lasted for forty years, until her death.

Da Ponte and his wife decided that their future lay in England rather than on the Continent, so they took up residence in London. Lorenzo had some difficulty in establishing his literary credentials at the start, but by the end of his first year he had managed to get himself appointed as poet of the King's Theater in the Haymarket. He tried to talk the theater director into staging *Don Giovanni*, but had to settle for a kind of potpourri of Don Juan musical settings by several composers, with Mozart being represented only by Leporello's "Catalogue" aria. Nancy da Ponte, an enterprising young woman, augmented the family income by taking over the refreshment concession in the lobby and operating it at a profit.

In 1798, the theater management sent da Ponte to the Continent to round up some singers for the coming opera season. He took Nancy with him, and the highlight of their visit was a reunion with his father Gasparo, né Geremia, now seventy-five years old and still living in Ceneda. The da Ponte clan had no idea it was their long-departed son who was knocking at their door one November evening, and they welcomed him with amazement and delight. The French poet Alphonse de Lamartine, who was fascinated by Lorenzo da Ponte and his adventures, wrote of this reunion: "Not even in the *Confessions* of St. Augustine, so tender and pious toward his mother, are there many pages of intimate literature superior to this return of a wandering son to the paternal hearth."

Da Ponte remained in London until 1805. Musical affairs at the King's Theater did not flourish, and to supplement his income he opened an Italian bookshop. At first it was so successful that he began to publish books himself, but this business, too, fell on hard times, and he was forced to close down. By now da Ponte was the father of four young children. His wife's parents had emigrated to America some time before, and he decided it would be best if Nancy and the children joined them there while he remained in London, at least for a time, in an effort to straighten out his financial affairs. This, however, proved a task beyond even his resourcefulness, and da Ponte learned from a friend that he was about to be arrested for debt. Carrying a minimum of luggage he forthwith headed for Gravesend, boarded a ship for Philadelphia, where his family had gone, and never set foot in Europe again.

Da Ponte's plan was to earn his living in the New World either by attaching himself to an opera theater as poet or by teaching Italian to the natives, but he quickly discovered that opera was nonexistent and that few Americans were desirous of Italian lessons. So on the advice of his father-in-law he went into the grocery business, first in New York City and then in Elizabeth (then called Elizabethtown), New Jersey.

Naturally, being da Ponte, he frequented whatever book stores and other literary establishments he could find. On a visit to one shop on lower Broadway in Manhattan he had a stroke of luck. He fell into conversation with another customer, a young man named Clement Clarke Moore, who was later to become famous as the author of the poem "A Visit from St. Nicholas," better known as "The Night Before Christmas."

The twenty-eight-year-old Moore was fascinated by the courtly and worldly Italian gentleman who was so familiar with classical literature. Moore was the son of Bishop Benjamin Moore, the president of Columbia College. He introduced da Ponte to his father, and both Moores decided to help him find pupils who wished to study foreign languages. The ever-helpful Nancy da Ponte soon was running similar classes for female students.

For reasons not altogether clear, Lorenzo gave up his teaching temporarily to try the grocery business a second time in Sunbury, Pennsylvania, where he also operated a transportation service consisting of a vehicle called "L. de Ponty's Wagon." Eventually, however, he returned to New York, and in 1825

Lorenzo da Ponte as he appeared in his prime in Vienna and in his old age in New York.

was appointed as the first Professor of Italian Literature of Columbia College—a title which, unfortunately, was principally honorary, since it was left to him to collect his fees from his students.

On the whole, da Ponte prospered reasonably well in his new country. He became a U.S. citizen in 1811 and—always adaptable to changing times and circumstances—established himself as a person of some importance and substance in literary and intellectual circles. He viewed himself as the unofficial ambassador of and spokesman for Italian culture in the United States, and his donations of books to the New York Public Library and to the Columbia library laid the foundations of the Italian collections of both institutions. He entered his oldest son, Joseph, as a student at Columbia, and he and Nancy turned their Manhattan home into a boarding house that became an informal center of European culture and refinement in the city. Da Ponte published translations of several of Byron's poems into Italian; he imported books from Italy in large numbers; and finally he wrote, from 1823 to 1827, a four-volume set of his *Memoirs* in which, unfortunately, he devoted less space to his recollections of Mozart than to his own escapades and constant endeavors to thwart, forestall, and triumph over his innumerable enemies.

Undoubtedly the supreme moment of da Ponte's life in America came on the night of May 23, 1826, when he heard, totally unexpectedly, a performance in New York City—the first ever—of *Don Giovanni*.

The artists were a group of singers from Spain led by the celebrated tenor Manuel Garcia. A Spanish Jew with an adventurous spirit not unlike da Ponte's own, the fifty-year-old Garcia arrived in New York with a company of singers including his twenty-year-old son Manuel and his seventeen-year-old daughter Maria, a contralto who was subsequently to become a world-famous prima donna under her married name of Malibran.

When da Ponte heard that a genuine European company was coming to present authentically Italian opera, until then a commodity totally unknown in New York, he was beside himself with joy. He rushed to the rooms where Garcia was staying and introduced himself. Garcia was astounded to discover the librettist of so many famous Italian operas living in New York; he grabbed the old man around the waist and danced him around the room singing "*Finch'han del vino*," Don Giovanni's "Champagne" aria, as he did so. Da Ponte for his part not only attended as many of the Garcia performances, given at the Park and Bowery theaters, as he could, but he got his Italian students to do likewise.

The Garcia company remained in New York for nearly a year, giving a total of seventy-nine performances. The main staple of their repertory was Rossini, including *The Barber of Seville* and *Otello*, but da Ponte suggested that they also put on "his" *Don Giovanni*. Garcia was amenable, but said he had no one to sing Don Ottavio, whereupon da Ponte not only went out and found him a suitable tenor but volunteered to pay his salary as well. Further, da Ponte had his son Lorenzo da Ponte, Jr., translate the words into English, engaged a printer to publish the Italian and English texts in parallel columns, and sold the librettos himself in the lobby.

In a preface he wrote, with unaccustomed modesty, of Mozart's operas: "The words of these dramas were written by me. All the glory owed to such miraculous works I gladly leave to that immortal genius. I merely beg to be allowed to hope that some little ray of that glory may fall upon me for having provided, with my fortunate poems, the vehicles for such eternal treasures."

The actual performance of *Don Giovanni* had its ups and downs. In the first-act Finale, with its tumultuous confrontation between the Don and his adversaries, the ensemble between singers and orchestra broke down so completely that Garcia, who was playing the Don, drew his sword, came forward, and stopped the performance, announcing it was wrong to so mistreat a masterpiece. He ordered everybody to pull themselves together and start again; and this time the scene was played to perfection, and to tumultuous applause. Thus did *Don Giovanni* receive its American premiere.

Nancy da Ponte died in 1831; she was sixty-two and Lorenzo eighty-two. Their most unlikely marriage had persisted and flourished. Lending substance to the story that they had been married as Jews was the fact that it was only after her death that Lorenzo made discreet inquiries about being received back officially into the Catholic fold. He finally succeeded in doing so, but only on his deathbed.

But even his beloved Nancy's passing did not deter him from the final mission he had set himself, of assuring the future of Italian opera in New York. To this end he persuaded a group of backers to erect a sumptuous opera house, complete with boxes and an ornate chandelier, on the corner of Church and Leonard streets in lower Manhattan. This elegant edifice was destroyed by fire only three years after being built. Da Ponte forthwith spent another two years busying himself with plans for a replacement, but on August 17, 1838, in his ninetieth year, he died, the last survivor of all the bright young men who had made music with Mozart at the court of Joseph II.

Da Ponte's mortal remains underwent a few adventures of their own. He was buried in a small diocesan graveyard on East Tenth Street in Manhattan. However, in 1909 the cemetery area was repaved for a playground, and the bodies there reinterred in Old Calvary Cemetery in Newtown, Queens. The gravestones were left in Manhattan and have been lost.

Unfortunately, da Ponte's new grave was—like Mozart's— never marked. In March 1985 an organization called the Native New Yorkers Historical Society decided to honor da Ponte's memory with a ceremony and wreath-laying at the approximate site in Old Calvary Cemetery.

"It was a rainy Sunday," recalls Felix Cuervo, president of the society. "The weather was miserable, damp, and chilly— the same as at Mozart's funeral. We were tempted to run for cover. But we wanted to sing something, and the only song we all knew straight through was 'O sole mio.' So we sang that."

Lorenzo da Ponte, a lover of irony, would have heartily approved.

Mozart and the Jews

"At present we are staying in places where there are four religions, Catholic, Lutheran, Calvinist and Jewish."

—Leopold Mozart, letter to Lorenz Hagenauer,
July 19, 1763

Lorenzo da Ponte was the best-known but by no means the only Jew to play a substantial role in Mozart's life. Jews were all but unknown in Salzburg, but when the Mozart family moved out into the world beyond they began encountering them, converted and otherwise. From the German town of Schwetzingen, the summer residence of the elector of Mannheim, Leopold Mozart wrote his friend Lorenz Hagenauer that among "the strange and unusual things" he was seeing on his travels were places with a multiplicity of religions, including the Jewish. Later on, in London, Leopold encountered a cellist named Emanuel Sipurtini. "This great virtuoso," he reported in some surprise, "is a Dutch Jew who finds the Jewish beliefs, ceremonies and commandments ridiculous." Leopold forthwith entered into an informal debate with Sipurtini and attempted to persuade him to undergo baptism. The cellist, however, dexterously evaded Leopold's proselytizing; he replied that he was content "to believe in one God, to strengthen that belief, to love his neighbor as himself, and to live as an honest man." Leopold gave up on converting him.

When Wolfgang settled in Vienna he found considerable numbers of Jews, most of them baptized, active in musical circles, though as patrons rather than as performers. Since Vienna was a cosmopolitan city, the capital of the Empire, their presence was not particularly surprising. Although there was no official ghetto, most of the Jews tended to congregate in one sector of the city, the crowded Leopoldstadt quarter. However, the relative few who had risen to wealth or found favor at court lived in more elegant areas.

Vienna in Mozart's time was hardly free of anti-Semitism; at best a feeling of ambivalence permeated the court. Maria Theresa, for example, conversed with Jewish supplicants when she had to, but she insisted on doing so from behind a screen. She also imposed restrictions as to Jewish property ownership, occupations, and activities. However, she forbade baptism of Jewish children contrary to the wishes of their parents. Many of her restrictive edicts were removed or eased by her son Joseph II, who regarded himself as a man of the Enlightenment. Most of the Jews Mozart knew were individuals who by dint of their commercial acumen had gained wealth, rank, and prestige and had either acquired official status as "protected Jews" or, more likely, undergone the conversion rite and in some cases even been elevated to the nobility.

Mozart seems to have gotten on uncommonly well with

such people. The one antagonistic remark in all his references to Viennese Jews came in a derogatory allusion to Eleonore Eskeles, the descendant of a chief rabbi of Moravia, who lived in Vienna with her brother, the banker Bernhardt Eskeles. Eleonore had been implicated in a spy scandal involving the turning over of imperial court secrets to the King of Prussia. Mozart took an interest in the affair because Eleonore was the mistress of a friend of his, Johann Valentin Günther, who was also involved in the scandal. In a letter to his father he spoke contemptuously of "the Jewess Eskeles . . . that sow." Eleonore was at first exiled from Vienna, but was later exonerated and returned to the capital. Mozart's resentment of her seems to have stemmed entirely from his friendship for Günther, by whom she had had two children. Of Judaism as such he appears to have known little; the closest he came to any commentary on the subject was to remark, speaking of an expected shipment of music: "I hope we shall not have to wait as vainly as the Jews for their Messiah."

Mozart was certainly no bigot, nor had he any reason to be. Music-loving Jews had a great deal to do with his success as a performer in Vienna and they also contributed substantially to his personal well-being. Their names are prominent on the list of subscribers he proudly sent to his father reporting on his series of three concerts in Trattner's Hall—Aichelburg, Arnstein, Henikstein, Sonnenfels, Wetzlar, and others. Joseph von Sonnenfels's collected writings made up one of at least two books by Jews in Mozart's personal library, the other being Moses Mendelssohn's *Phaedon*, an updating of Plato's philosophy and one of the most popular literary works of the time.

Among Vienna's Jews Mozart's closest friend and most faithful supporter was Baron Raimund von Wetzlar, after whom Wolfgang named his first child. Wetzlar, whom Mozart met shortly after his arrival in Vienna, was the son of Karl Abraham Wetzlar, a native of the town of Offenbach in Hesse. The senior Wetzlar emigrated to Vienna where he became a banker and was elevated to the nobility with the title of Baron von Plankenstern after accepting baptism. Both of the Wetzlars admired Mozart's music, the older attending some of his earliest concerts in Vienna while the younger became his close friend and helped him out with loans and gifts. On one occasion, when Mozart wished to give a private ball for his friends, Raimund von Wetzlar placed some empty rooms at his disposal. He also attended the party, which must have been a good one, since it lasted from six in the evening until seven the next morning.

Wetzlar's greatest assistance to Mozart came when he gave Wolfgang and his new bride lodgings in his house and refused to accept any rental; later on, when he needed the rooms, he found the Mozarts other lodgings, again free, and even bore the moving expenses himself. Wetzlar and Mozart remained friends to the end of Wolfgang's life; no supporter, except perhaps Michael Puchberg, was as loyal and as generous.

Mozart's original intention had been to name his first child Leopold or Leopoldine in honor of his father, who was still very much alive. However, when a son was born he suddenly decided to give Wetzlar the honor of standing godfather. In a rather tortuous letter he explained to his father that Wetzlar, "a good and true friend of mine," had offered to be godfather, and he hadn't been able to refuse him. The boy who, as it turned out, lived only a few months, was accordingly named Raimund Leopold. One can picture the skepticism with which Leopold Mozart received his son's labored explanation.

One curious aspect of the christening of little Raimund Leopold is that Wetzlar himself did not appear at the ceremony. Instead he had a stand-in at the baptismal font, Philipp Martin, the impresario who was presenting Mozart in a series of indoor and outdoor concerts. Wetzlar's failure to attend the religious ritual raises the possibility that, unlike his father, he may not have actually undergone conversion. In later years he became one of the founders of a new synagogue in Vienna. His wife, Joanna Theresa von Picquigny, was also of Jewish origin, being the daughter of a French convert. Wetzlar's mother, a baroness, always refused to accept conversion.

It was at Raimund Wetzlar's home that Mozart met Lorenzo da Ponte. In his *Memoirs* da Ponte describes "Baron Vetzlar" as Mozart's "great admirer and friend" and reports further that Wetzlar was instrumental in bringing about the creation of *The Marriage of Figaro*. He even offered to pay for the libretto himself and to see to it that the work would be produced either in Paris or London if by any chance a Viennese performance were prohibited for political reasons. The musicologist Paul Nettl has expressed the belief that it was Wetzlar who directed the attention of both da Ponte and Mozart to Beaumarchais's *Le Mariage de Figaro* as an operatic possibility in the first place.

Most of the other Jews Mozart knew in Vienna were members of the Masonic lodge he joined in 1784. Anti-Semitism was minimal in the Masonic lodges of the day. Several Masonic brothers from other cities actually signed the visitors' book of Mozart's lodge in Hebrew; among them was Wenzel Tobias Epstein, a government functionary from the Tyrol, who inscribed a quotation from the Mishnah. Epstein, who became a member of the lodge, wrote a preface for one of Mozart's Masonic compositions, the cantata *Die Maurerfreude* (K. 471). Wolfgang obviously felt at home in the company of men who knew no religious barriers.

Not until the advent of the Nazis upon the European scene did a "Jewish question" arise regarding Mozart and his music.

Actually, the Nazis' involvement with Mozart was relatively light; the two composers they were chiefly concerned with were Wagner, whom they raised to the level of a demigod, and Mendelssohn, whom they tried to expunge from musical history. However, not even Mozart, as apolitical as any musician who ever lived, completely escaped their ministrations. In 1937 the Nazi cultural authorities discovered that the standard translations of Mozart's Italian librettos into German were the work of Hermann Levi, a Jew, and they forthwith ordered that these be scrapped. New translations into "Aryan German" were ordered from one Sigrid Arnheisser.

The Nazis also interfered with the work of the Mozarteum, the great musical and educational institution established in Salzburg in 1841. Following the *Anschluss* of 1938, the Nazis disbanded its entire board of directors and removed Bernhard Paumgartner, the head of its conservatory since 1917, because he was Jewish. The Nazis apparently were trying to reduce the Mozarteum to the status of a local establishment; they made it call itself the "Stiftung [Foundation] Mozarteum" rather than the "Internationale Stiftung Mozarteum" and they substantially limited its activities. Their objective seemingly was to have Mozart students from Europe come to Berlin for their studies rather than Salzburg.

None of these changes survived the war; Paumgartner was reinstated in 1945 and continued his distinguished career as a musicologist and conductor until his death in 1971. Today the Mozarteum flourishes as the world's preeminent institution devoted to Mozartean research and scholarship.

Mozart's Religion

Whoever wanders this path of affliction
Will be purified by fire, water, earth and air.
If he can overcome his fears of death
He will soar from earth Heavenward.

—*The Magic Flute*, Act II

What, exactly, were the religious beliefs of Wolfgang Amadeus Mozart? It is not an easy question to answer, for in the course of his life he was both a Catholic and a Freemason, experiencing the often contradictory pulls of traditional tenets and beliefs and the lure of the inquiring and rationalistic attitudes of the spreading Enlightenment in Europe.

Mozart was born a Catholic and remained one all of his life; he never did or said anything that indicated the least dissatisfaction or doubt with established religion. Nevertheless, he had little regard for churchmen; considering his humiliating experiences at the hands of Archbishop Hieronymus Colloredo it would have been remarkable if he had felt otherwise. The household in which he was raised was thoroughly Catholic, although Leopold himself, while accepting God's will, had no objection to offering the deity some human assistance from time to time. Leopold repeatedly urged his son to fulfill "the duties of a true Catholic Christian" with diligence. "You know me," he said. "I am no pedant or praying Peter and still less a hypocrite. But surely you will not refuse a father's request that you take thought for the welfare of your soul so that in the hour of his death you may cause him no anxiety, and in that dread moment he will have no reason to reproach himself for not having cared for your soul's salvation."

Wolfgang himself, especially during his younger years, gave his father little cause for concern on religious grounds. "God is ever before my eyes," he wrote in response to Leopold's adjurations; he attended mass and went to confession, he married within the church and had no thought other than to raise his children as good Catholics. Peter Winter, the German composer who detested Mozart, once mocked him for letting his moral scruples prevent him from taking a mistress. "You're earning enough," he told him. "What's stopping you? Your religion?"

More than once Wolfgang gave a religious expression to his feelings of gratitude. When his Paris Symphony, K. 297, was to be played at the Concerts Spirituels, he promised to say the rosary if it succeeded, and he did so, although, as he wrote to Leopold, not before stopping off for "a large ice" at a café in the Palais Royal. When his bride-to-be Constanze fell ill shortly before their marriage he vowed to compose a mass if she recovered; the result was the Mass in C minor, K. 427.

Despite the grandeur of the C minor Mass and the dark

beauty of the Requiem (both of them unfinished), liturgical music does not play a really major part in Mozart's output. There is considerable charm in his early masses and other choral pieces written, for the most part, while he was in Salzburg. But his most perfect church piece is the less-than-five-minute-long "*Ave, verum corpus,*" which he composed in 1791, six months before his death. This work for four voices, strings, and organ was composed for a little parish church at Baden, where Constanze had been taking her medicinal baths. It was a thanks-offering to the choirmaster, Anton Stoll, who had been helpful to Mozart's wife during her visits to the spa, and who often performed his music at the church. Some time before, Mozart had become acquainted with the music of Johann Sebastian Bach, then rarely performed, at the home of his friend Baron Gottfried van Swieten, and the great contrapuntalist's influence may be sensed in this compact, close-textured miniature masterpiece.

From a purely personal standpoint, Mozart's religious sensibilities might have seemed perfectly conventional had he not, during his Vienna years, become an active and ardent Freemason. It is somewhat difficult for us today, when Freemasonry is regarded as essentially a fraternal, charitable, and social organization, to picture the controversial role it played in eighteenth-century religious and intellectual affairs. The Masonic lodges had been first established in England in 1717, and spread through much of Europe, reaching France in 1725 and Austria in 1742. The Freemasons were a secret society in that they had their own rituals and symbols, but they were hardly the sinister organization sometimes depicted by their enemies. Far from being anti-religious, they accepted members of all faiths and professed a belief in God, whom they chose to characterize as the "supreme Architect" of the world. They preached human brotherhood and equality, thus participating in the growth of the spirit of liberalism that pervaded the late eighteenth century.

Whether because of the Freemasons' insistence that religion was strictly a private concern of each individual, or their general air of secretiveness, the order aroused the suspicion and hostility of the Catholic church, and in countries like Spain and Italy Masonry was banned. Curiously, the order attracted the adherence of a good many members of the nobility, who were perhaps eager to show that they, too, had been touched by the Enlightenment. Francis I, the husband of Maria Theresa, was a Mason, although after his death she promptly declared the society illegal. However, her son Joseph II lifted the ban when he succeeded her, and during the 1780s the Freemasons of Vienna flourished in numbers and expanded in influence.

Mozart joined the lodge called *Zur Wohlthätigkeit*, or Beneficence, on December 14, 1784. Many of his friends belonged to the lodge, and he himself brought in new members, including his father, during his visit to Vienna, and Joseph Haydn.

Neither Leopold Mozart nor Haydn was ever more than a nominal Mason, but Wolfgang became deeply involved in the affairs of his lodge. He attended meetings regularly, participated in the rituals and, most importantly of all, wrote a good deal of music, some of it of great nobility, to accompany Masonic ceremonies and express Masonic ideals.* He accepted the fellowship and ethical code of Masonry with the same sense of devotion he had brought in earlier years to the spiritual warmth and comfort of Catholicism. But he did not abandon the one for the other; six months before his death he marched in a

---

*One factor in Mozart's affinity for the Masons may have been the enthusiasm and respect with which they accepted his music—so different from the attitude of many other Viennese. When his lodge Beneficence was merged into a lodge called Newly Crowned Hope (*Neugekrönte Hoffnung*) he wrote a celebratory cantata that was received with such acclaim that he observed: "How madly they have gone on about my cantata! If I did not know that I had written better things, I should have thought it my best composition."

Billboard for the first performance of *The Magic Flute* at the Theater auf der Wieden. The name of the librettist, Emanuel Schikaneder, is displayed far more prominently than Mozart's.

Trinity Sunday church procession in Vienna holding a lighted candle in his hand. It is interesting to speculate what he might have done had he lived in a country where a choice between the church and the order was necessary.

Masonic symbolism is discernable in other works besides Mozart's lodge music. It appears most notably in his last operatic masterpiece, *The Magic Flute*, which depicts a mysterious Eastern order dedicated to brotherhood and lofty ideals under the tutelage of a beneficent, almost godlike seer named Sarastro. Various efforts have been made by scholars to associate specific Masonic personalities and even musical sequences with *The Magic Flute*, and there seems no doubt that the opera would have been quite different in both its setting and its music had Mozart not been a Freemason. But whether *The Magic Flute* is purposefully a "Masonic opera" may be questioned. It was, after all, a "magic opera," a farrago of various comic and sober elements, and it would have been perfectly natural for Mozart to incorporate into it whatever ingredients lay conveniently at his hand without being too concerned with hidden meanings and secret symbols.

As Mozart grew older and suffered bouts with illness and despondency his religious thoughts grew increasingly fatalistic. When he heard in April 1787 that his father was seriously ill (Leopold died the following month) he wrote:

> I need hardly tell you how much I long to hear better news from you. And I anticipate it, though I am now in the habit of being ready for the worst in everything. Since death, when we really think about it, is the true goal of our existence, I have formed in the last few years such close relations with this best and truest friend of mankind that his image no longer terrifies me, but actually soothes and consoles! And I thank my God

for graciously granting me the opportunity (you know what I mean)* of learning that death is the *key* which unlocks the door to our true happiness. I never lie down at night without reflecting that—young as I am—I may not live to see another day.

Apparently Mozart's prominence in the ranks of the Free-masons was looked upon with disfavor in church circles. As he lay on his deathbed in December 1791, his sister-in-law Sophie Haibel set out for St. Peter's Church in Vienna to seek a priest to administer extreme unction. For whatever reason, none she could find seemed anxious to come to the stricken composer. Sophie herself remembered years afterward: "The priests hesitated a long time and I had great difficulty in persuading one of these inhuman priests to do it."

After his death, it was the Masonic mourners rather than the Catholic who paid the fittest tribute to Mozart both as a man and as a musician. An elaborate memorial ceremony was held a few days after his funeral at the Newly Crowned Hope lodge, with the grand master, Karl Friedrich Hensler, delivering the eulogy:

> It has pleased the Eternal Architect of the World to separate from our fraternal chain the most beloved and meritorious of its members. Who did not know him? Who did not esteem him? Who did not love our worthy brother Mozart? Only a few weeks ago he was still among us, and exalted with his enchanted sounds the dedication of our Masonic temple. . . . Mozart's premature death represents an irreplaceable loss for Art—

*Apparently an allusion to Mozart's Masonic affiliation.

his talents, already expressed in early boyhood, made him even then the rarest phenomenon of his generation; half of Europe revered him, the great called him their favorite, and we, we called him our Brother. . . . Brotherly love, a peaceable disposition, support of good causes, . . . these were the chief characteristics of his nature. . . . He was a husband, a father, a friend to his friends, a brother to his brothers. . . .

> *With gentleness and patience*
> *A Mason heart and soul*
> *He lifts our aspirations*
> *Towards a higher goal.*

How Mozart Composed

"I would rather neglect playing the clavier than neglect composing."

—Mozart, letter to his father,
February 7, 1778

In his short lifetime, Mozart wrote more than 600 numbered compositions as well as others that have been lost—a tremendous output by any standard and almost incredible when one considers its quality. Yet not very much is known about how he worked or the mental and physical aspects of his creative process.

Obviously he was a fast worker; otherwise he could hardly have written so much. Music was almost always in his mind; he composed at meals, while socializing with his friends, while playing billiards, while traveling in a stagecoach. Sometimes when an idea for a piece seized him he could not rest until it was finished; on other occasions he could be indolent, deferring a commissioned work until the last minute. His letters home from Vienna abound in excuses for tardiness in delivering promised scores.

Mozart was preeminent among the school of composers who first think out music in their heads, then write it down on paper. He usually didn't even bother to try out his ideas at the piano. That, at least, is the image conveyed by Constanze Mozart, who said: "He wrote down music in the same way as he wrote letters." The most celebrated story of Mozart's ability to create an entire work intact in his mind relates to the Overture to *Don Giovanni*, which was written down on paper on the night before the opening performance, so that the musicians had to play it from sight without any rehearsal. However, such a procedure may have been more commonplace than one might suppose. A generation later Gioacchino Rossini was writing overtures exactly the same way. When a fellow-composer asked him about the proper method of writing such pieces, Rossini advised: "Wait until the evening before opening night. Nothing primes inspiration better than necessity, whether it be the presence of a copyist waiting for your work or the prodding of an impresario tearing his hair. In my time, all the impresarios in Italy were bald at thirty."

Mozart himself once wrote to his sister that he was distressed by the "laboriousness" of writing out strings of notes, and that he often sat down at the keyboard to "play fugues out of my head," only writing them down when importuned to do so. He was a master of improvisation which, after all, is a form of impromptu composition. One of his early biographers, Adolph Heinrich von Schlichtegroll, reported that at a court concert Mozart sat down in an ensemble about to play one of his works with a blank sheet of paper in front of him. "Where is your part?" Emperor Joseph II asked him in astonishment. "Here," replied Mozart, touching his forehead. Once Mozart had completed writing down a work he rarely made changes, unlike— to cite one contrast—Beethoven, who was forever tinkering with and improving his pieces.

And yet there are indications that Mozart's ability to compose was not as facile as it might appear, that for him writing music could be hard work, not merely a matter of switching on a computer in his head. Nor was he completely free of the need of a piano to try out his ideas; during their trip to Paris his mother reported back to Leopold that Wolfgang spent a good deal of his time composing at the home of Jean Le Gros, the director of the Concerts Spirituels, because he had the use of a keyboard instrument there. Several sketches exist of compositions that Mozart actually worked out on paper, among them his fine piano concerto No. 23 in A, K. 488. Erasure marks are visible in the minuet of his first string quartet in G, K. 80, which he wrote in an inn in the town of Lodi at the age of fourteen on his first trip to Italy. We still have fragments of a number of movements he began and then discarded, for whatever reason. Probably many other sketches and rough drafts were made and are missing; for him there was no reason to save such scraps once he decided not to proceed.

However, there is no doubt that Mozart is unmatched for his sheer ability to plan, conceive, and bring to fruition great music in his mind, if need be without the aid of writing material or a performing instrument. This isn't to say that his music ever was purely cerebral or divorced from practical considerations. Mozart was a thoroughgoing professional; he wrote to order, according to the terms of the commission, the availability of the performers, and the needs and tastes of the audience.

He was particularly careful to tailor his music to the ability of the artists at his disposal. "I like an aria to fit a singer as perfectly as a well-made suit of clothes," he wrote to his father while he was working on his opera *Idomeneo*. The singer in question was Anton Raaff, the tenor way past his prime who was singing the title part.

And yet he was equally insistent upon his singers performing in such a way that they conveyed both the situations and the personalities they were to depict upon the stage. Enamored as he was of Aloysia Weber, he did not neglect to instruct her in the psychological niceties of a concert aria of his designed for Andromeda, the mythological beauty rescued by Perseus from a sea-monster: "I advise you to watch the expression marks, to think carefully of the meaning and significance of the words, to put yourself as seriously as you can into Andromeda's situation and plight, to imagine that you really are that very person."

Mozart was also careful to write instrumental music that would not only convey the desired emotion but would capitalize upon the strong points of his performers: Most of his piano concertos were designed either with himself in mind, or for his pupils or others who had requested them, such as the blind virtuosa Maria Theresa von Paradis. His Concerto for Two Pianos, K. 365, was written for himself and his sister. He always was on the lookout for top-notch performers, and it is striking how many of them were women, including his pupils Barbara Ployer and Josephine Aurnhammer. In 1784 he wrote to his father from Vienna: "The famous Strinasacchi from Mantua, a very good violinist, is now here. She has a great deal of taste and feeling in her playing. Right now I am composing a sonata which we are going to play together." The reference was to Regina Strinasacchi, an Italian virtuosa, and the work he wrote was the Piano and Violin Sonata in B-flat, K. 454, one of his most brilliant pieces in the form. At the actual concert, which was attended by the emperor, Mozart typically played his own part from his head, having written down only Strinasacchi's. Only afterward did he write out the piano part. Incidentally, Leopold Mozart shared his son's enthusiasm for female performers. After hearing the same Strinasacchi play the following year in Salzburg he wrote to Nannerl: "In general, I think that a woman who has talent plays with more expression than a man."

Sometimes a performer even managed, without knowing it, to impart his own personality to a piece. Mozart had a friend named Ignaz Leutgeb who had been a horn player in the Salzburg orchestra. Later he relocated in Vienna, where to support himself he opened a cheese shop while still taking what we should now call free-lance engagements as a hornist. Mozart, naturally, bought his cheeses from his old friend, whom he apparently regarded with a kind of good-natured contempt. Mozart wrote at least three horn concertos for Leutgeb, taking full advantage of his agility on the instrument to make him play all sorts of skips, leaps, and flourishes. To underscore his friendly mockery he wrote one of the concertos in multicolored inks and filled the margin with such comments as (before a particularly difficult passage) "*Corragio!*" and, at the end, "Thank Heavens! Enough, enough!" One wonders if Leutgeb's cheeses were as zesty as Mozart's music.

Mozart enjoyed musical humor, and never more so than in a piece he actually entitled *Musikalischer Spass—A Musical Joke* (K. 522). This was a sextet for strings and two horns which satirized the work of inept or amateurish composers, of whom there undoubtedly were a good many in Vienna at the time. The themes are trite, development sections lead nowhere, the accompaniment chugs along mindlessly, the first violin goes off in a mad cadenza that winds up with a pointless pizzicato note. The entire piece ends in disarray with three horrible discords. The parody is delightful to listen to for its own sake, but it also is an object lesson in how *not* to compose. Curiously, a few weeks later Mozart composed, almost as a countermeasure, one of the most exhilarating and bracing of his own serenades, the famous *Eine kleine Nachtmusik*, K. 525.

Mozart composed concertos or sonatas for virtually every instrument except the violoncello, which had to be content with an unusually strong part in the three string quartets known as the *King of Prussia* Quartets, K. 575, 589, and 590. The Prussian King, Frederick William, to whom they were dedicated, played the cello, and Mozart certainly was not going to overlook a detail like that in planning the works.

Mozart also wrote solo music for instruments that were complete novelties and that he must have known were unlikely to enter the musical mainstream. Two of these were pieces for "clock-work organs," elaborate mechanical devices popular at the time. There also were two works, K. 617 and K. 617a, involving the "glass harmonica."

This was an instrument invented by none other than Benjamin Franklin. When he arrived in England as American envoy he found "musical glasses" all the rage. These consisted of drinking glasses filled with water to various heights. When one "played" them by rubbing one's moistened fingers along the edges they gave off ethereal musical tones. Characteristically, Franklin made a genuine musical instrument out of them by connecting thirty-seven glasses by rods to a central mechanism that was revolved by a foot-treadle. He called his device, which had a span of three octaves, the "armonica," but to the British it became better known as the "glass harmonica" or "glassy-chord." For a time it had a considerable vogue, one of its best-known exponents being a blind performer named Marianna Kirchgässner, for whom Mozart wrote his two pieces.

Mozart's operas, of course, were written on commission; there was never a question of composing one first and then looking around for someone to produce it. Even *La finta semplice* (*The Pretended Simpleton*), composed at the age of eleven, stemmed from a request by Joseph II, who was curious to see what sort of an opera a child could write. In his operas, Mozart invariably kept his audience as well as his singers in mind, yet he never compromised his artistic standards or his musical ideas. Perhaps he expressed his outlook best when he said that he had written his opera *Don Giovanni* a little for Prague (the city that had commissioned it), a little for his friends, and a little for himself. Sometimes his operas proceeded on two levels—one for audiences that appreciated graceful melody and charming harmony without going very much beyond these surface attractions, the other for listeners who could grasp deeper musical significances. Both *The Magic Flute* and *Così fan tutte* are instances of such twin-tiered masterpieces. Mozart himself was well aware of the challenge of pleasing both the uninitiated and the sophisticated musical listener. Of one of his piano concertos he wrote: "There are passages here and there from which connoisseurs alone can derive satisfaction, but these passages are written in such a way that the less learned cannot fail to be pleased, though without knowing why."

For many years such popularity as Mozart's operas retained was due largely to the beauty of individual arias or an occasional duet. Don Giovanni's "Champagne" aria, Figaro's "*Non più andrai,*" Susanna's "*Deh! vieni, non tardar,*" Sarastro's "*In diesen heil'gen Hallen,*" the "Letter" duet from *The Marriage of Figaro* and the ever-radiant "*Là ci darem la mano*" duet from *Don Giovanni*—it was "numbers" like these that kept audiences listening in the opera houses of the nineteenth century. But in more recent years appreciation has grown for Mozart's ensembles, those episodes in which many characters are upon the stage, with the composer developing their dramatic and musical destinies with incomparable mastery. When the Mozart Opera Society of England made its first recordings of *The Marriage of Figaro* in 1934, they were not of the arias and other "famous" parts, but of the ensembles, such as the wonderful twenty-minute-long denouement of Act II. It was only afterward that the complete opera was recorded for the first time.

Similarly, modern listeners have become aware of the wealth of beautiful detail in the orchestral parts of Mozart's operas. Even in his own time many listeners found such music rather too rich for their tastes. Musicians who should have known better were disturbed, as witness the criticism of his French contemporary, André Grétry, who complained that while most composers placed the statue on the stage and the pedestal in the orchestra, Mozart placed the statue in the orchestra and the pedestal on the stage—meaning that too much action was taking place in the orchestration.

Unfortunately the provenance of much of Mozart's music is not known, even though in midcareer he began keeping a catalogue of his compositions, starting with the Piano Concerto No. 14, written for Barbara Ployer, who, he remarked to his father, had paid him "handsomely" for it. Despite the labors of musicologists and scholars, the dates, places, and circumstances of a number of Mozart's compositions, including some of the most celebrated, have never been definitively determined. There even is an air of uncertainty about the great triumvirate of symphonies—the E-flat, K. 543, the G minor, K. 550, and the *Jupiter*, K. 551. We know from his catalogue that they were composed within seven weeks in the summer of 1788 (perhaps the most concentrated production of a series of masterpieces in musical history) but there is no actual record of their having been performed anywhere until after his death.

Mozart enjoyed listening to his own works, and he had his favorites among them. In 1784 he reported to his father that he thought his Quintet in E-flat for Piano and Winds, K. 452, was "the best work I have ever composed," although many he wrote in subsequent years must surely have surpassed it in his mind. When he heard his woodwind Serenade in E-flat, K. 375, played to him by "six poor wretches" outside his door in Vienna, he went into ecstasies of delight. Michael Kelly reported him standing in the wings at the dress rehearsal of *The Marriage of Figaro* listening to the baritone Francesco Benucci singing Figaro's stirring aria *"Non più andrai"* and calling out—like any other spectator—"Bravo! Bravo, Benucci!" Kelly also recalled that Mozart had a particular favorite in the *Figaro* score—the delightful sextet in which Figaro discovers that Bartolo and Marcellina really are his long-lost parents. And, after attending a performance of *The Magic Flute*, Mozart wrote to his wife: "You have no idea how charming the music sounds when you hear it from a box close to the orchestra—it sounds much better than from the gallery."

One Mozartean favorite that the composer never mentions but that plays a curious part in his life's work is a four-note theme (the sequence is C-D-F-E) which recurs in a surprising number of his pieces. It appears in the Andante of his very first symphony in E-flat, K. 16, composed in London at the age of eight; in his Symphony in B-flat, K. 45b; in the Credo of his Missa Brevis in F, K. 192, composed in Salzburg in 1774; in the Sanctus of the Mass in C, K. 257. Later works that have it include the Symphony No. 33 in B-flat, K. 319; the Violin Sonata in E-flat, K. 481; and, most gloriously of all, his final symphony, the *Jupiter*, No. 41 in C, K. 551, where it constitutes the opening motif of the great fugal Finale.

No one knows the significance of this almost mystical musical motto, which is said to be derived from an ancient church tune, or why Mozart should have kept reverting to it in so many works. Mozart's "theme song" remains one of the intriguing musical mysteries of his life.

The Medical Mozart

"Josef, there's nothing doing today; today we're going to be occupied with doctors and apothecaries."

—Mozart to Josef Deiner, November 1791

Music-lovers are not notably more morbid than other folk, yet many are peculiarly fascinated by details of the illnesses and deaths of their favorite composers. Were Beethoven and Schubert really afflicted with syphilis? Did Tchaikovsky bring on his death by drinking unboiled water during a cholera epidemic? What sort of insect bite caused the blood poisoning fatal to Alban Berg? Answers to questions like these may never be answered with finality, yet they continue to engage the attention of medical and musical sleuths.

Of all such mysteries, the circumstances leading to the death of Wolfgang Amadeus Mozart are the most fascinating and puzzling. Partly this is because he died at such an early age and after such a period of great productivity; partly because he lived in an atmosphere of rivalry and intrigue; partly because rumors that his death was not natural began to spread soon after his burial and have been reflected in works of art from Pushkin's 1830 poetic drama *Mozart and Salieri* to Milos Forman's 1984 Academy Award–winning movie *Amadeus*.

Certainly for a man who lived only to the age of thirty-five Mozart compiled an active medical history. He was well acquainted with physicians and it may be significant that those he portrays in his operas (Bartolo in *Figaro* and the doctor impersonated by the maid Despina in *Così fan tutte*) are figures of burlesque.

Both Wolfgang and his sister Nannerl appear to have been blessed with reasonably robust constitutions; after all, they were the only two of the seven children in the family to survive infancy. According to Mozart himself, all were raised on sugar water rather than on mother's milk. This was a fairly common practice at the time; Mozart thought it was a highly satisfactory method, for he told his father that he wanted his first child nourished the same way but had to give up on the idea because "the people here [i.e., Vienna] don't know how to do it properly."

That both Wolfgang and Nannerl survived their arduous childhood travels is an indication of their inherent healthiness, for they certainly were exposed to every affliction from seasickness to smallpox. A portrait of Wolfgang painted at the age of six shows him a well-proportioned if smallish youngster with bright eyes and rosy cheeks. During the family's three-year trek through Europe and England he was smitten with a succession of childhood diseases including colds, rashes, and fevers that sometimes necessitated the cancellation of scheduled appearances. At the age of eight he came down with scarlet fever.

In London it seems to have been Leopold himself who was the chief sufferer, from respiratory diseases, while in the Hague Nannerl fell ill with typhoid, developing a fever so severe that Leopold actually feared she would die. No sooner had she recovered, after a long siege, than Wolfgang was stricken with the same illness, lying incapacitated for four weeks until, according to his father, he was left with nothing but "his tender skin and little bones." The family returned safely to Salzburg, but took a trip soon after to Vienna, where they found a smallpox epidemic under way. Leopold immediately hustled them all off to Olmütz in Moravia; it was too late, however, and both children came down with this disease. Fortunately the attacks were fairly light and each was left with only a few pockmarks.

To treat any and all of the diseases that struck his family, Leopold Mozart's universal remedy was "black powder" and herb tea. The nature of the powder is not known. Wolfgang vainly tried to obtain some when his mother lay ill in Paris, but reported to his father that no one there had ever heard of it "even under the name of *pulvis epilepticus*," apparently its generic appellation.

During his years of adolescence and young manhood Mozart's health seems to have been tolerably good, although at the age of sixteen, according to a letter written after his death by Nannerl, he suffered an illness that caused him to look "sickly and yellow" for a time. The first truly alarming medical episode of his adulthood occurred at the age of twenty-eight in Vienna when he was taken ill while attending a performance of Giovanni Paisiello's opera *Il rè Teodoro in Venezia* and wound up with cramps and vomiting that went on for nearly a week. He was put under the care of Dr. Sigmund Barisani, whose family Wolfgang had known in Salzburg and who had recently set up shop in Vienna. Barisani's diagnosis was that Mozart had received a "chill on the kidneys"—the first indication of the condition that most medical authorities today believe led eventually to his death. Barisani and Mozart became good friends; the doctor inscribed a poem in an album Wolfgang kept, praising him as matched in composition only by Hadyn and Bach—although he undoubtedly meant Johann Christian Bach rather than Johann Sebastian. Barisani, who became chief physician at the General Hospital in Vienna, died in 1787 at the age of twenty-nine. Mozart was grief-stricken and inscribed a brief note in his album, under the poem Barisani had written there, describing him as a "noble man, dearest and best of friends, and the preserver of my life."

Barisani had evidently attempted to direct Mozart into more healthful paths and a more regular lifestyle. It's conceivable that a billiard table Mozart owned—exceeded in cost among his possessions only by his piano—was acquired in response to Barisani's advice that he needed regular recreation. In any case, following Barisani's untimely death Mozart does not seem to have had a personal physician, nor to have practiced any particular health regimen. Nevertheless, his health remained on a fairly even keel for several years—or perhaps the medical problems of the rest of the family gave him no time to worry about his own.

On May 28, 1787, Leopold Mozart died in Salzburg at the age of sixty-seven. Wolfgang had heard a report that his father was ill and wrote to him in early April, asking for further information about his condition so that if it were truly serious "I may come to your arms as quickly as humanly possible." Constanze was going through a difficult spell at the same time and had to be bled, so Wolfgang had other cause to be distraught. When he received the actual news of Leopold's death he was writing a note to one of his patrons, Baron Gottfried von Jacquin, to accompany some scores he had promised, and added this footnote: "I inform you that on returning home today I received the sad news of my beloved father's death. You can imagine the state I am in." Despite the change in their relations Wolfgang and his father had maintained a steady correspondence and Leopold's death inevitably had a depressing effect upon him.

Wolfgang's own health took a turn for the worse around the middle of 1790; he had rheumatic pains, headaches and toothaches, and was plagued by business problems as well— when he tried to enlist a group of subscribers for a new concert series he came up with only one name, that of Baron Gottfried van Swieten. By October Mozart felt well enough to undertake a trip to Frankfurt where Leopold II, who had succeeded Joseph II, was having his coronation ceremony. Not being part of the official retinue, Mozart had to raise money for the trip, which he did by pawning the family silver plate. He returned without having noticeably improved his fortunes or restored his health.

Although in his last year Mozart produced some of his greatest masterpieces, including his Piano Concerto No. 27 in B-flat, K. 595, his beautiful little motet "*Ave, verum corpus*," K. 618, his Clarinet Concerto, K. 622, and his opera *The Magic Flute*, his health gradually deteriorated, despite periods when he seemed to be in relatively good shape.

A number of curious and unexpected events took place during 1791. Apparently one more serious attempt was made to induce Mozart to go to England to compose operas, with Lorenzo da Ponte involved in the negotiations, but, perhaps with his health in mind, Wolfgang declined.

In May an old acquaintance turned up with an unusual commission. This was Emanuel Schikaneder, an erstwhile boy violinist who had turned actor and become the director of his own theatrical troupe. Mozart had originally met Schikaneder, four years older than himself, years before in Salzburg, where

Emanuel Schikaneder costumed as Papageno in *The Magic Flute*.

the actor had arrived with his traveling company and presented the Mozart family with free tickets to his shows, including plays by Shakespeare, Molière, and Goethe. In return Wolfgang had composed an aria for use in one of his musical productions.

Schikaneder, a flamboyant, picaresque character, had a repertory that included plays like *Hamlet* and *King Lear* (with himself in the title roles of both), and he also dabbled in musical extravaganzas. Now he told Mozart that he had taken over the huge, barnlike Theater auf der Wieden on the outskirts of Vienna, where he wanted to put on a German-language "magic opera"—that is, a musical show with an exotic story, fantastic settings and costumes, spectacular stage effects, animals, and plenty of comic scenes for himself. Mozart accepted the commission, but he had his reservations. "If we make a fiasco I cannot help it, for I never wrote a magic opera in my life," he said.

Schikaneder evidently had a few doubts, too, not about the idea of the opera, but about Mozart's ability to get it completed in time. He knew of Wolfgang's habit of not writing things down until the last minute, and presumably was not unaware of his health problems. So he installed his composer in a little summer house in a courtyard adjacent to the theater where he could keep an eye on the progress of the music. He also endeavored to keep up Mozart's spirits by taking him off on drinking bouts from time to time.

Hardly had rehearsals of *The Magic Flute* begun in July when even a more surprising commission arrived. This came from a mysterious stranger representing an anonymous client who wanted a requiem mass, to be delivered as quickly as possible. Mozart began working on it but had to put it aside after completing a substantial portion because still another rush job came his way. His old friends in Prague, for whom he had written *Don Giovanni*, decided at the last minute that they wanted him to compose an opera to celebrate the coronation of Leopold II as king of Bohemia.

Unfortunately they presented him with an ancient and creaky libretto adapted from Pietro Metastasio's *La Clemenza di Tito*, a work about royal generosity, which they regarded as appropriate to the monarchical festivities. Mozart always was a fast worker, but his pace now became feverish. He composed *La Clemenza di Tito* in eighteen days, utilizing the assistance of his pupil Franz Xaver Süssmayr. Although it has been revived with some success in recent years, at its premiere it was a total failure, with Empress Maria Luisa, herself of Italian background, calling it *"una porcheria tedesco,"* a piece of German swinery.

Mozart resumed working on the Requiem when he returned from Prague; indeed, he had little choice, because the stranger who had ordered it kept coming back to inquire when it would be ready. After several such calls, and with his inability to discover who had commissioned the work, Mozart apparently became possessed of the idea that he was being asked to compose his own death music. Actually the mysterious emissary was the steward of a certain Count Franz Walsegg-Stupach, who had the curious habit of commissioning well-known composers to write music, copying it out in his own hand, and then passing it off as his own in private performances on his estate. Earlier that year the count's wife had died, and it was to memorialize her that he had ordered a requiem from Mozart. The work was not actually performed until December of 1793, with Walsegg himself conducting; by then its true authorship had become widely known.

None of this, of course, was ever known to Mozart, who went to his death oppressed by the urgency and mystery of this last commission. He worked at the Requiem almost desperately, plagued by fainting spells, headaches, vomiting, and swelling of his hands and feet. From time to time he improved a little; he was able to conduct the first two performances of *The Magic Flute* himself.

The symptoms of his illness were apparent even to casual acquaintances. In November he stopped into the Silver Snake tavern, an establishment frequented by musicians and theater people, to order some firewood from Josef Deiner, the waiter there. Deiner told him that he didn't look well, and asked him jokingly whether he had upset his stomach drinking too much beer in Prague during the *La Clemenza di Tito* premiere. "My stomach is better than you think—I've learned to swallow all sorts of things," was Mozart's bitter reply. He also told Deiner he felt a chill coming on and that he couldn't finish the glass of wine that had been placed in front of him. The next day Deiner called to deliver the wood, and was told that Mozart was sick in bed and that it had been necessary to call a doctor during the night.

What was ailing him? The official diagnosis was "heated miliary fever," a now obsolete term that occasionally is misprinted as "military fever." The word *miliary* derives from papules or vesicles resembling millet seeds; skin eruptions were among Mozart's symptoms. The truth is that the doctors of the time didn't know for certain what he died of, and physicians ever since have been arguing about it. The most commonly accepted diagnosis of today is uremia following chronic kidney disease, with the hectic, punishing pace he set himself during his last year as a possible contributory factor. In support of this theory are such medical events as Mozart's childhood attack of scarlet fever and his many subsequent infections and sore throats, which in certain cases can lead to or be accompanied by acute inflammatory or suppurative damage to the kidney. Another possible analysis, advanced by Dr. Carl Bär in Switzerland during the 1960s, is that the composer's underlying illness was rheumatic fever.

In any event Mozart spent the last two weeks of his life in bed, with doctors marching in and out of the house. He had two of the best in Vienna, Dr. Nikolaus Closset, who had become the family physician, and Dr. Mathias von Sallaba, chief of the General Hospital. They could only provide palliatives, such as putting cold compresses on his head, and told Constanze and her younger sister, Sophie Haibel, for whom Mozart had developed a particular affection, that his case was hopeless. Sophie made a nightshirt for him that could be put on from the front since it was difficult for him to turn his swollen body; she also took a songbird from the room because its sounds disturbed him.

To the end, his mind was on his music. *The Magic Flute* by now was a tremendous hit, filling Schikaneder's theater night after night, and Mozart would keep an open watch on his pillow following its performance minute by minute in his mind. Once he told his wife he should have liked to have heard the opera once more, and began to hum Papageno the bird-catcher's song. A friend who was in the sickroom went to the piano and played it for him.

He also kept working on the still-unfinished Requiem with Süssmayr at his bedside, explaining in detail how he thought it should be completed. There even was an informal rehearsal session of the Requiem in his room at 2:00 P.M. on December 4, a Sunday, with three of his friends joining in. Benedict Schack, the first Tamino, sang the soprano part; Franz Hofer, his brother-in-law, the tenor; Mozart himself the alto; and Franz Xaver Gerl, the first Sarastro, the bass, with Süssmayr at the clavier. When they came to the Lacrimosa Mozart broke down and wept, and they did not go on. In the evening he became unconscious and that night, at 12:55 A.M. on December 5, 1791, Mozart died, aged thirty-five years, eleven months, and nine days.

Mozart and Salieri

"I shall tell you when we meet of Salieri's plots."

—Mozart, letter to Michael Puchberg,
December 29, 1789

Many celebrated composers—Purcell, Pergolesi, Schubert, Bellini, Mendelssohn, Bizet, Gershwin—have had their lives cut short, yet Mozart is the only one whose early death was regarded as suspicious by his contemporaries. Rumors of foul play began to circulate almost immediately. On December 31, 1791, a Berlin weekly musical journal reported: "Because his body swelled up after death, some people believe that he was poisoned." A number of theories were set forth at the time—and have been since—as to who the poisoner might have been, but the most frequently mentioned suspect was Antonio Salieri, court composer to Emperor Joseph II and one of the best-known musicians of his time.

Salieri, five years older than Mozart, was a skilled and prolific composer, but more importantly, he was a consummate politician who ran the musical life of Vienna for more than half a century. In his worldly success he surely must have been an object of envy to Mozart as well as to dozens of other composers working at the Hapsburg court.

Salieri was born August 19, 1750, in Legnano, near Verona, the son of a well-to-do merchant. Orphaned at the age of fifteen, he went to Venice for musical studies, and there met Florian Gassmann, an accomplished operatic composer. When Gassmann later moved on to Vienna, he took Salieri, whom he regarded as his most promising pupil, with him. Gassmann, who eventually was appointed court composer in Vienna, introduced Salieri around, encouraged him musically, and saw to it that he learned languages and polished his social graces. This was all done to such effect that when Gassmann died in 1774, the Emperor appointed Salieri to succeed him as court composer, making him, at age twenty-four, the dominant figure in Vienna's musical life.

The young transplanted Italian seems to have gotten on perfectly well with most of the musicians working in Vienna. He was on good terms with Haydn, Beethoven, and Schubert (the latter became his devoted pupil), all of whom held him in high regard. But with Mozart an animosity set in early—almost as soon as Wolfgang settled in the capital. Mozart's letters abound in digs at Salieri; soon after his arrival in Vienna he wrote to his father in exasperation that he had been all set to give piano lessons to the Princess of Wurttemberg only to learn that the emperor had suggested she first consult Salieri. "Why, Salieri is not capable of teaching her the clavier!" Wolfgang wrote bitterly. "All he can do in this business is to try to injure me by recommending someone else." A few years later when Lorenzo da Ponte promised to write an opera for him, Mozart's comment was: "If he is in league with Salieri, I shall never get anything out of him." In other letters he described Salieri as an "enemy" and denounced his "tricks," while Leopold Mozart, for his part, advised his daughter that he had heard Salieri was leading a "cabal" against *The Marriage of Figaro* and would "again move heaven and earth" to assure its failure. Even a somewhat more neutral observer was wary of Salieri, for the singer Michael Kelly characterized him as "a clever, shrewd man possessed of what Bacon called 'crooked wisdom.'"

Salieri and Mozart often found their operas vying with each other for places on the court theater schedule, and on one occasion were actually pitted in direct competition. In January 1786 Joseph II gave an elaborate court entertainment at Schönbrunn Palace in honor of his sister Archduchess Christine Marie, who together with her husband governed the Austrian Netherlands. Although Joseph regarded himself as a follower of the Enlightenment, he knew how to stage a typical *ancien régime* festivity. Although only eighty guests were invited, the Orangerie, a huge, glass-covered enclosure filled with orange trees, was specially heated upon a wintry day and an elaborate banquet served to the music of a wind-band. Two stages illuminated by candelabra had been built at either end, and on these the emperor ordered that two short new operas, one in Italian by Salieri, the other in German by Mozart, be presented in turn. Mozart, who had to interrupt his work on *The Marriage of Figaro* to comply with the royal request, responded with *Der Schauspieldirektor* (*The Impresario*), a piece about a producer desperately trying to pacify two squabbling sopranos. Salieri's effort was a work with the intriguing title *Prima la musica e poi le parole* (*First the Music and Then the Words*), which deals with the contention between a composer and a librettist who have been commissioned to produce an opera in a hurry.

MOZART AND SALIERI

It is curious that both Mozart and Salieri should have written works dealing with theatrical backstage problems. Mozart's cast also is of interest; his two battling prima donnas, Mme. Herz and Mme. Silberklang, were played by Aloysia Lange, his old girlfriend, and Catarina Cavalieri, Salieri's mistress. The operatic twin bill at the Orangerie was not officially designated as a contest, so there was no question of declaring a winner. However, it may be significant that Joseph ordered a payment of 100 ducats ($1,250) to Salieri and only 50 to Mozart. One Vienna newspaper did publish a review saying that "the German piece (i.e., Mozart's) infinitely surpassed the Italian one in intrinsic value." However, the ultimate verdict was given, as always, by posterity, for the *Schauspieldirektor*, a well crafted and charming work, is still produced, while *Prima la musica*, like the rest of Salieri's enormous musical output, has all but vanished.

In retrospect, Salieri's high reputation as a composer in his own time is puzzling, for his music, for all its facile mastery of eighteenth-century forms and styles, seems thin in content and substance. None of his forty operas is ever given today, and when an instrumental piece of his does appear on a concert program it generally is to provide a contrast with something of Mozart's. Yet in his own day he was admired not only in Vienna but in Paris, Milan, Venice, and Naples, where his operas were welcomed enthusiastically.

After Mozart's death Salieri's career continued to flourish. In 1824, the fiftieth anniversary of his appointment as court composer was the occasion of a great celebration during which pieces by his pupils, including Schubert, were performed. When he died the following year all of musical Vienna turned out for his elaborate funeral.

Salieri never wrote down his feelings about Mozart, so we do not have his side of the antagonism between them. It seems

187

Antonio Salieri. An engraving made in 1802.

certain that it existed on both sides—the question is why. Some have argued that Salieri resented his fellow composer's superior talents, but there is little indication that Salieri was sufficiently perceptive—as, for example, Haydn was—to recognize the true depths of Mozart's genius. Besides, Salieri really had little to fear; his own operas were successful everywhere, he had practically been anointed as the musical heir of Gluck, his supremacy at court was unchallenged. He could easily have afforded to be generous to Mozart, and he was not: that really is the chief crime he committed.

Toward the end of Mozart's life the relationship between the two composers appears to have been undergoing a change for the better. Salieri evinced great interest in *The Magic Flute*, which had made such an unexpected success at the Theater auf der Wieden. He wanted to see the new work and, hearing that he wanted to go, Mozart invited him to his own box. With Salieri came his mistress Cavalieri. "You cannot imagine how pleasant they were and how much they liked not only my music but the libretto and everything," Mozart wrote to Constanze, who as usual was taking the baths at Baden. "They both said it was worthy to be performed at the grandest festival and for the greatest monarch, and that they would see it many times again, as they had never seen a more beautiful or delightful show." There seems no reason to doubt the genuineness of Salieri's praise: Mozart watched him closely throughout the performance and observed him following attentively and with pleasure from start to finish. Curiously this letter (October 14, 1791) is the last to have been written by Mozart.

Salieri's liking for *The Magic Flute* perhaps stemmed from the fact that it is, after all, a German rather than an Italian opera, the latter being his own specialty; or perhaps from a realization that Mozart was no longer a threat to him. Or perhaps—the most reasonable explanation of all—he simply fell, as so many others have since, under the spell of this unique masterpiece, at once charming and exalting. In any case, it is an intriguing thought that Mozart and Salieri might have drawn closer had Wolfgang lived.

Why, then, did stories begin to circulate that Salieri had poisoned Mozart? No one could say then, and no one can say now. Salieri had a reputation as an intriguer, and some of Mozart's symptoms were consistent with poisoning. But that is a long way from adding up to credible evidence.

The closest we have to a "documentary" indication of foul play is a statement that Mozart's widow made to Mary Novello when the British music-lover came to call on her in 1829.

Manuscript of the Piano Sonata No. 8 in A minor, K. 310, which Mozart wrote in Paris a few days after his mother's death.

According to Constanze, Mozart became possessed with the idea that he was being poisoned six months before his death. His exact words, as she recalled them, were: "I know I must die —some one has been giving me aqua toffana."

Aqua toffana was a slow-acting, transparent, odorless poison with an arsenic base that had a reputation in the eighteenth century as a favorite device of would-be murderers. It drew its name from Teofania di Adamo, a seventeenth-century Italian woman from Salerno, who allegedly invented it, dispensed it in vials during her lifetime, and passed the formula down to others.

It is entirely possible that Mozart, troubled as he was by illness and despondency, really believed that poison was being administered to him; on the other hand, it must be remembered that Constanze's statement to Mary Novello was made nearly forty years after Wolfgang's death, when she was sixty-six years old and had had plenty of opportunities to absorb the rumors that had circulated through the years.

Constanze never mentioned Salieri as a suspect. After all, she had permitted her second son, Franz Xaver Wolfgang, to take lessons with Salieri, which she hardly would have done had she believed he poisoned her husband. Franz Xaver, for his part, once expressed the view that while Salieri had not murdered his father he had "truly poisoned his life with his intrigues" and that this burden was always on his conscience.

Salieri outlived Mozart by thirty-three years, dying at the age of seventy-four. The accusation that he was responsible for his rival's death reached his ears and may have played a part in a mental collapse he suffered in his seventies. He is said to have gone to his death avowing "I did not poison Mozart." On the other hand he also reportedly said: "It is a pity to lose so great a genius but his death is just as well for us. If he had lived, not a soul would have given us a crust of bread for our work."

The true tragedy of Antonio Salieri is that his name lives on in musical history only by reason of his association with Mozart. His works died with him. W. H. Auden wrote his proper epitaph in his poem "Metalogue to The Magic Flute":

> *We should,*
> *As Mozart, were he living, surely would,*
> *Remember kindly Salieri's shade,*
> *Accused of murder and his works unplayed.*

The list of candidates accused of the poisoning of Mozart does not end with Salieri; in fact it grows increasingly bizarre the further one pursues it. An English writer named Francis Carr has suggested, not very convincingly, that the culprit was Franz Hofdemel, the lodge brother of Mozart who believed his wife Magdalena was having an affair with the composer. In 1953 Igor Boelza, a Soviet musicologist and former editor of *Sovietskaya Musica*, set forth the startling theory that while Salieri did the actual poisoning, the plot also involved a cover-up involving, among others, Mozart's friend and patron Baron van Swieten. According to Boelza, van Swieten had Mozart buried in an unmarked grave because he feared the working class of Vienna would have risen in revolt against the nobility had it known that its beloved composer had been a victim of intrigue at the imperial court.

This Marxist interpretation is more than matched by a Nazi theory ascribing Mozart's death to a Masonic-Jewish conspiracy. The fullest elaboration of this hypothesis came from General Erich Ludendorff, the German World War I commander who became an early supporter of Adolf Hitler, and his wife Mathilde Ludendorff, also an ardent Nazi. In 1926 Ludendorff wrote an article alleging that the Freemasons had poisoned Mozart to punish him for writing an *anti*-Masonic opera in *The Magic Flute*. "The secret of Masonry is the Jew," he wrote. "Freemasonry has tried to rob the German people of their Germanic pride." Ludendorff's wife Mathilde, the holder of an MD degree, carried the campaign further, publishing in 1936, when the Nazis were firmly in power, a book entitled *Mozart's Life and Violent Death*. In it she charged that the Masons, including Salieri, van Swieten, and the anonymous messenger who commissioned the Requiem, had poisoned Mozart because he had revealed the order's secret rituals in *The Magic Flute* and also because he held pro-German views. The Freemasons, it may be remembered, were banned by the Nazis, although this action had nothing to do with Mozart's murder, real or supposed.

Jealousy, politics, religion, nationalism—all of these have been cited as possible motives for the poisoning of Mozart. Against such legends the simple diagnosis of kidney trouble seems unspeakably prosaic and dull. Nevertheless it remains the most plausible explanation of what really killed Mozart.

Mozart's Mourners

"There is no shadow of death anywhere on Mozart's music. Even his own funeral was a failure. It was dispersed by a shower of rain; and to this day nobody knows where he was buried or whether he was buried at all or not. My own belief is that he was not. Depend on it, they had no sooner put up their umbrellas and bolted for the nearest shelter than he got up, shook off his bones into the common grave of the people, and soared off into universality."

—Corno di Bassetto (George Bernard Shaw),
The Star, May 16, 1890

At Mozart's funeral all the ingredients were in place to create a legend of an unappreciated genius buried in a mass pit without a friend or relative willing to brave a winter storm to follow him to his pauper's grave. That tale has been destroyed, or at least amended, by recent scholarship. Yet in some ways the truth of what happened, so far as we know it, is even more puzzling than the traditional version accepted for more than a century and a half.

The date of the funeral itself is in dispute. For years it was generally accepted that Mozart was buried on December 6, 1791, the date listed in the Register of Deaths of St. Stephen's Cathedral in Vienna. However, in 1967 Dr. Carl Bär, in a book* published with the blessing of the Mozarteum in Salzburg, concluded that the funeral had actually taken place a day later. Bär based his finding largely on the statement of Josef Deiner, the steward of the Silver Snake tavern, who was called in to dress Mozart's body after death. Deiner gave the funeral date as December 7 in his *Memoirs*, which were not, however, published until 1856, sixty-five years after the event.

Along with the question of the date goes a controversy over the weather. Was the winter storm at the time of the funeral real or imaginary? In 1960 the musicologist Nicolas Slonimsky hit on the brilliantly simple idea of checking the meteorological records of the city of Vienna for December 6, 1791, the traditional date of the funeral, and found that it had been "a relatively mild day that could have prevented no one from marching all the way to St. Mark's Cemetery and throwing a handful of earth on Mozart's grave—if he so wished." Confirming this was an entry for that date of Count Karl Zinzendorff, a leading Viennese diarist: "Mild weather and frequent mist."

Carl Bär similarly consulted the weather records of the Vienna Observatory for December 7, and found that neither rain nor snow had fallen on that date, but that there had been

*Bär's book, as yet untranslated into English, is entitled in German *Mozart: Krankheit—Tod—Begräbnis.*

high winds, which conceivably could have deterred mourners from following the hearse from the church to the cemetery, a distance of about two and a half miles. As against these meteorological records there remains Deiner's assertion, in 1856, that "rain and snow fell" at the time of the funeral and that the few mourners "stood around the bier with their umbrellas." Yet if precipitation had occurred in the city one would surely expect it to be noted in the official records. The absence of any such indication for either the sixth or the seventh strongly suggests that Deiner was exaggerating any inclemency of the weather or that his memory was playing him tricks.

However, Deiner's date of December 7 for the funeral is gaining increasing acceptance among musical historians. Among the arguments in its favor is that it reflects a Viennese public health requirement at the time that a waiting period of forty-eight hours be observed between certification of death and actual burial. The purpose was to prevent premature interment, the only exceptions permitted being for Jews, whose religion demanded prompt burial, and for victims of contagious diseases. Had Mozart been buried on December 6, the forty-eight-hour waiting period would have been ignored.

Further perplexity centers around the cheapness of the funeral. It was not literally a pauper's burial (which would have been free) but a third-class funeral, the cheapest available, costing less than 12 florins, or about $30. Deiner's report says that the formal religious ceremony took place in a small "outside chapel" behind the cathedral, half in the open air. Carl Bär disputes this, arguing that the ceremony was performed in a small chapel, but indoors, and the body only afterward was transported to the outdoor chapel to await conveyance to the cemetery. Whichever report is correct (and no one can ever know), there is no doubt that the ceremony was minimal, if not perfunctory.

Bär also contends that most of the other aspects of Mozart's funeral that posterity has found distressing—such as burial together with other bodies—were merely reflective of Viennese funeral practices of the time. He notes, for example, that 80 percent of the paid funerals in Vienna around the time of Mozart's were of the third-class variety.

Nevertheless, it seems evident that with a greater effort and a slightly increased expenditure Mozart could have had a more dignified and impressive funeral, including even a grave of his own. He was not, after all, among the 80 percent of ordinary citizens, but a prominent musician of the court, an admired composer, a great pianist, and, ever since his prodigy days, a celebrity of European renown. Particularly if the actual burial took place on December 7, there was plenty of time to prepare a worthy rite. That this was not done remains an eternal reproach to his patrons, friends, and family.

Constanze herself did not make the arrangements; she was absolutely stunned by Mozart's death and became distraught and hysterical, with the result that she, her elder son, and her six-month-old baby were all quickly removed to a friend's house. The person who made the decisions about how and at what cost Mozart should be buried was his friend and patron, Baron van Swieten. Why he was selected is not known; perhaps he was the only one of Mozart's well-connected friends who could be quickly reached, or perhaps he volunteered his services.

Van Swieten was one of the most active, and also one of the most idiosyncratic musical worthies of Vienna. The son of a Dutch father who had been Maria Theresa's personal physician, van Swieten had a connoisseur's taste and plenty of money with which to indulge it. He had a particular discernment for the music of such past masters as Johann Sebastian Bach, whose music was little known to the public, and George Frideric Handel. But he also seems to have been something of a prig who cultivated, in the words of one contemporary, "only the great and exalted." He had himself composed a dozen symphonies which Joseph Haydn irreverently said were "as stiff as himself." Van Swieten had his own system of silencing people who talked at concerts: "If it chanced," one observer noted, "that a whispered conversation began, His Excellency, who was in the habit of sitting in the first row, would rise solemnly, draw himself up to his full height, turn to the culprits, fix a long and solemn gaze upon them, and slowly resume his chair. It was effective, always."

Van Swieten's musical tastes could tend to the peculiar. He had introduced Mozart to the music of Bach and Handel, which was all to the good, but he had also induced him to provide a new, elaborate, and totally unneeded orchestration for Handel's *Messiah*. It also was he who insisted that Haydn imitate the croaking of frogs in his oratorio *The Seasons*. Haydn subsequently apologized for the sounds of "this wretched conceit," but he owed a debt to van Swieten, who actively propagandized for the work. The baron also helped the young Beethoven, who dedicated his Symphony No. 1 in C to him in 1801.

Mozart, then, was only one among many "great and exalted" composers whom van Swieten befriended. But the baron certainly did a botched-up job on his funeral. A few extenuating circumstances may be cited. He evidently was trying to save money for Constanze. He also could have argued that the arrangements he ordered were in keeping with austerity customs introduced by Joseph II and still in effect. Finally, he had other things on his mind: the day before he had been notified that he was being dismissed by the new emperor, Leopold II, as president of the Court Commission on Education, a position he cherished.

Nevertheless, certain things are hard to explain. Although

according to Wolfgang's sister-in-law Sophie Haibel, "crowds of people walked past his body and wept and mourned for him" on December 5, while he was laid out in his own home, hardly any mourners appeared at the actual funeral service, and none at all, whatever the reason, went to the cemetery. Those who did attend the service at the church included Salieri, van Swieten, Mozart's pupil Süssmayr, and Deiner, the faithful steward of the Silver Snake. Some accounts report that a few women and several Masons were also present, but there is no agreement as to their identity.

Even more inexplicable than this feeble showing was Constanze's failure to have a monument erected for her husband. Within a week Mozart's wife had regained her composure sufficiently to apply to Emperor Leopold II for a court pension (which she eventually got), but she never pulled herself together enough to return to the cemetery, seek out the unmarked grave, and arrange for a cross or another marker to be placed above it. Her subsequent explanation that she thought such matters were handled automatically by the church parish does not sound very convincing. A marble stone monument was not erected at St. Mark's Cemetery until December 5, 1859, and its proximity to Mozart's actual resting place was sheer guesswork.

In the aftermath of Mozart's death his Requiem took on new significance to Constanze, not because of his obsession that he had been writing it for himself, but for a more practical reason: his widow could not receive the final payment until it was delivered to the mysterious emissary who had commissioned it. Mozart had died before its completion and, not wishing to hand over an unfinished manuscript, Constanze decided to find someone to fill in the missing parts.

She first asked Joseph Eybler, the Vienna court conductor, but he declined, so she turned to Franz Süssmayr, Mozart's pupil. Süssmayr was no novice; he was twenty-five years old, had written the recitatives for *La Clemenza di Tito*, and had worked closely with Mozart on the Requiem, presumably being privy to the composer's plans for completing it. An added strength —at least so far as Constanze was concerned—was that he could imitate Mozart's musical handwriting. Süssmayr shrewdly capped his deception by completing the work with the repetition of a fugue used earlier—a device that Mozart had employed in his earlier masses. He did his work so well that scholars and musicians have been wrangling inconclusively ever since over which portions of the Requiem are Mozart's and which Süss-mayr's.

Obituary notices and testimonials for Mozart were not slow in coming in. Some of the most sincere emanated from Czech and Hungarian sources. In Prague, a city which had taken Mozart to its heart as none other, a memorial service and concert were held on December 14; a vast throng converged on St. Nicholas's church, which held only 3,000, so that 2,000 more stood in freezing cold in the square outside. Some of the obituary articles that appeared made allusions to Mozart's financial state; one Vienna newspaper commented that he had suffered from "that indifference to his family circumstances which so often attaches to great minds" and that he "could have, nay should have, earned riches for such famous works."

Of all the ironies associated with Mozart's death, none is more bitter than that it occurred just when those riches and rewards almost seemed within his grasp. Mozart himself seemed to realize that, all too late, his prospects were brightening. One of his first biographers, Franz Xaver Niemetschek, in a book published in Prague in 1808, reports him saying on his deathbed: "I must go just at the time when I could live in peace! I must now leave my art when I, no longer the slave of fashion, no longer bound by speculators, would be free to follow the promptings of my sensitivity, could write freely and independently what my heart tells me! I must leave my family and my poor children at the moment when I would be in a position to care better for their welfare!"

Whether or not Mozart used the exact words ascribed to him, he had justification for such hopes. He had received promises of commissions from patrons in Hungary and Holland; his English friends were trying to arrange guaranties for a trip to London. It was not merely a matter of money but of ever-widening recognition, as became evident when his very death unloosed a tide of appreciation for his music that had been lacking before.

With no other work was this more evident than with *The Magic Flute*, which ran on and on at the Theater auf der Wieden until it attained a total of 223 performances in ten years. Theaters

Mozart's sons Karl Thomas (left) and Franz Xaver Wolfgang. Both died unmarried and without issue.

in other towns took it up, and soon it was playing all over Europe, especially in German-speaking lands. It became, as record producers say nowadays, Mozart's greatest hit.

A typical account of *The Magic Flute*'s popularity may be found in a letter Johann Wolfgang von Goethe received from his mother in 1793, two years after Mozart's death. Writing from Frankfurt, she reported: "There is no news here but that *Die Zauberflöte* has been given eighteen times, and that the house is always packed full; no person will have it said of him that he has not seen it; all the artisans, the gardeners, even the inhabitants of Sachsenhausen, whose children play the apes and lions, go to see it. A spectacle like this has never been known here before; the house has to be opened before four o'clock each time, and in spite of that some hundreds always have to go away again because they cannot get a seat—all this has brought in a lot of money!"

How Mozart would have gloried in this letter, could he have seen it! Undoubtedly, much of *The Magic Flute*'s success on the stage was (and is) due to its broad comedy, its magical settings, its cavorting animals. But more than any other opera by Mozart, indeed, more than any opera by *anybody*, it combines and unites a frankly popular musical style with one that expresses the deepest ethical convictions. And Mozart, too, in his frail and fragile person, embodied man's earthy and spiritual elements in their fullest measures. Perhaps that is why *The Magic Flute*, written in the last year of his life, is a truer monument to him than a stone upon his grave.

Mozart's Cataloguers

"Madame Mozart of Vienna, the composer's widow, has sold to me the whole of the manuscripts of her husband that remained in her possession. I am thus in a position to produce the most accurate edition of several works of our beloved Mozart, both known and unknown."

—Johann Anton André, January 31, 1800

Only 144 of Mozart's more than 600 compositions were printed during his lifetime. After her husband's death Constanze Mozart found herself with a mass of unpublished manuscripts ranging from fragments and sketches to fully completed works. Although she was musically literate she obviously needed expert help in organizing and evaluating them with an eye to doing justice to Mozart's reputation, not to mention assuring an income for herself. For several years she did nothing except sell off a few pieces, but eventually she got down to the serious task of sorting and arranging his music.

For assistance she turned to Abbé Maximilian Stadler, an Austrian priest, composer and scholar, an old friend of the

Typical pages of Mozart's own thematic catalogue. The left-hand page describes each work, while the right gives its opening measures. The first entry listed here is the Piano Concerto in D Major (K. 537) completed on February 24, 1788.

Mozart family who had settled in Vienna in 1796. Constanze offered to send the manuscripts and other material for examination to Stadler's lodgings, but the abbot, not wanting to risk losing them, preferred to work in her house. By now Constanze was living with Georg Nikolaus von Nissen, who eventually became her second husband. Nissen, a Mozart enthusiast, lacked

the technical knowledge to do the cataloguing himself, but he eagerly assisted Stadler.

They had certain guideposts to work with, one being a list compiled by Leopold Mozart in 1768. Mozart's father had been upset by allegations that his son was not the real composer of the opera *La finta semplice* and accordingly recorded everything Wolfgang had written so far. This first Mozart listing was headed:

> Catalogue
> of all that this 12-year old boy
> has composed since his 7th year
> and can be shown in *originali*.

Also of great use was Mozart's own *Verzeichnüss aller meiner Werke*, a catalogue he began on February 9, 1784, with the Piano Concerto No. 14 in E-flat (K. 449) and continued until three weeks before his death, his last entry being the Masonic cantata, "*Laut verkünde unsre Freude*" ("Loudly Announce Our Joy"), K. 623. In the little leather-bound notebook Mozart entered the title and date of each work in one column at the left and the opening measures on the right. Sometimes he made mistakes in dates, and he omitted about twenty works. The catalogue totalled 176 compositions, and there were twenty-nine blank pages remaining in the book when he died. The title page is particularly poignant, for Mozart had pasted on it a piece of paper reading: "All my works from the month of February 1784, to the month of 1   ." In leaving space for the second date Mozart did not include the projected termination year as 17—, but as 1 __, indicating that he expected to live into the 1800s. After all, he was only twenty-eight when he started the catalogue.

Stadler went through the manuscripts, relating those that he could to the two catalogues and trying to put all of the others in some semblance of systematic order. "I read everything out," he later reported. "Herr Nyssen [*sic*] carefully wrote every-

Georg Nikolaus von Nissen, Constanze's second husband.

thing down, and we quickly brought the catalogue into being." Altogether they found 280 compositions unlisted by either Mozart or his father. There also were a number of fragmentary pieces, and Stadler undertook to complete some of these himself.

With the cataloguing completed, Constanze had hopes of finding a publisher to purchase the entire collection of manuscripts from her. Breitkopf & Härtel at first expressed interest, but they wound up accepting only a handful. It was not until 1875 that this foremost of German music publishers finally brought out its complete Mozart edition.

However, an enterprising young man named Johann Anton André, who had just inherited his father's music publishing business in the town of Offenbach, now entered the picture. Joseph Haydn, ever eager to promote Mozart's music and to assist his widow, told André the collection was available. After some negotiations with Constanze, he purchased the entire batch for 3,150 gulden (over $15,000). André was far more than an entrepreneur out to make a quick return; he loved Mozart's music, and the more he studied the manuscripts the more caught up in them he became. Some he published; others, which he held back because he believed the market was not yet ready, he kept locked in a cabinet under controlled atmospheric conditions. Toward the end of his life, he became concerned about the eventual disposal of the collection and offered to sell it intact to several libraries and public institutions in Vienna, Berlin, and London. None of them wanted it, and after his death in 1842 the manuscripts were distributed among his heirs. Finally in 1873 the Prussian State Library purchased those scores that were still held by family members, but by then some manuscripts had fallen into other hands. However, it is thanks to André's perceptiveness and persistence that so much of Mozart's music has been preserved in its authentic form.

The name that has become imperishably associated with Mozart's music—specifically with its numbering—is not however André's, but that of Ludwig Alois Friedrich von Köchel. Not a musician but a botanist by profession, Köchel constitutes an excellent instance of how progress in a specialized field can be provided not by an expert in that area but by a person of broad, general culture. Born in Stein, a town forty miles from Vienna, Köchel earned a law degree, worked as a tutor, and branched off into botany and mineralogy. There even is a plant named for him, the *Bupleurum Koechelii*.

Köchel was a musical amateur with a particular affinity for Mozart. Around 1850 he decided to undertake the task of compiling an accurate, authoritative, and exhaustive catalogue of Mozart's output, arranging the works in strictly chronological order, which had never been done before. Establishing the chronology was no simple matter, for many pieces were undated. To do so Köchel relied on internal evidence, such as musical style and the handwriting of a given composition. In each case he gave the first few bars of the music, assigned a number, and listed the manuscript source. Fragmentary or doubtful works were included in an appendix. Not least important, Köchel finally induced Breitkopf & Härtel to utilize his catalogue, printed in 1862, for publication of a definitive edition of all of Mozart's music. However, public interest in the composer had begun to decline, and by 1883 Breitkopf & Härtel obtained fewer than 100 subscribers, including seven in the United States, for the complete set.

Köchel himself died in 1877. At his funeral Mozart's Requiem was performed. Many changes have been made in the "Köchel Catalogue" since his death; newly discovered works have been added; dubious compositions either authenticated or rejected. The most thoroughgoing revision was that undertaken by Dr. Alfred Einstein, published in 1947, which has been the basis of all subsequent editions.

But Ludwig Köchel's "K numbers" have never been abandoned, and remain indelibly attached to Mozart's output, from K. 1, a Minuet and Trio for Piano composed at age five, to K. 626, the unfinished Requiem.

Mozart and the Romantics

"Romanticism proper did everything possible to misinterpret Mozart in terms of itself, since it could not deny his existence; but a few Romantic musicians nevertheless understood how to amalgamate some part of the essential Mozart with their work."

—Alfred Einstein, *Mozart* (1945)

At the start of the nineteenth century the romantic movement became a flood tide carrying on its crest whatever suited its style and spirit, but submerging everything else. It is sometimes forgotten how quickly events moved and styles changed in that tumultuous era. Fifteen years after Mozart's *Jupiter* Symphony came Beethoven's *Eroica*, and only six years after that Berlioz's *Symphonie Fantastique*. "Modern music" in the generation after Mozart's death meant Beethoven, and the audience, for the most part, accepted it rapturously. Beethoven's achievement would not have surprised Mozart, for he is reported to have said, when the newcomer from Bonn was brought to him for a hearing in 1787: "This young man will make his mark in the world." Mozart, as we know, was not always so generous in his estimate of newcomers.

The tremendous impact made by Beethoven coincided with—and perhaps to a considerable extent was responsible for—the emergence of the symphony orchestra as the supreme vehicle of musical expression in the world, a position it retains to the present. From this point on, symphonic and operatic composition began to take divergent paths, with composers generally concentrating on the one or the other.

Mozart, of course, had excelled in both, but it is striking that the romanticists fastened on only a few of his works in each form. Felix Mendelssohn, one of the most intelligent and cultivated musicians of the nineteenth century, deeply admired Mozart. Yet when he conducted concerts with his Leipzig Gewandhaus Orchestra and other groups he concentrated on a handful of Mozart pieces, all of which suited the romantic susceptibilities of the time. Mendelssohn's favorites were the Piano Concerto No. 20 in D minor, with himself playing the solo part,* the Symphony No. 40 in G minor, and the Concerto for Two Pianos in E-flat, which he played with Ignaz Moscheles —a performance one would give much to have heard. Similarly *Don Giovanni* was the only Mozart opera Mendelssohn ever conducted. Such selectivity disturbed sensitive musicians like Johannes Brahms who remarked: "The fact that people do not

---

*Beethoven also particularly admired this concerto; he even composed cadenzas for it.

understand and respect the very best things, such as Mozart's concertos, is what permits men like us to become famous."

To nineteenth-century romantics, *Don Giovanni* became a heroic figure to a degree that Mozart could hardly have imagined, let alone intended. After all, he had adopted the subject of the great lover simply because da Ponte had suggested it for the new opera commissioned by Prague in 1787, and the story was well-known and handy. But to the romantics, Mozart's Don Juan quickly effaced all previous versions of the old Spanish saga. Lord Byron, whose own epic satirical poem *Don Juan*, written from 1818 to 1823, has certain Mozartean resemblances, even echoes in one of his letters Leporello's "Catalogue" aria describing the Don's conquests. To a friend inquiring about his own love affairs in Italy Byron wrote inquiring which lover he meant, explaining: "Since last year I have run the gauntlet: Is it the Taruscelli, the Da Mosti, the Spineda, the Lotti, the Rizzato, the Eleanora, the Carlotta, the Giulietta . . . ," and so on for another dozen names. Byron, like Leporello, kept a list.

Another who took up *Don Giovanni* as a literary theme was the Danish philosopher Sören Kierkegaard who in 1843 offered his analysis of the character in an essay entitled "The Stages of the Erotic or the Musical-Erotic." Kierkegaard's essay, which many readers may be forgiven for finding impenetrable, is built around the theme that "Don Juan is actually neither Idea— that is, Power, Life—nor Individual; he hovers between both." Once again, Mozart might have found this complicated psychological exegesis hardly what he had in mind when he wrote his opera.

Of all the subsequent tales, poems, essays, and other literary manifestations evoked by *Don Giovanni* the most romantic is a spooky story by E. T. A. Hoffmann entitled "Don Juan, or a Fabulous Adventure that Befell a Music Enthusiast on His Travels."

MOZART AND THE ROMANTICS

Ernst Theodore Wilhelm Hoffmann, who lived from 1776 to 1822, was a German writer, composer, and jurist with a vivid imagination and a taste for strong drink, his favorite libation being a mixture of cognac, arrack, and rum which he called "punch." He once wrote out a list of musical recommendations for tipplers: "Rhine wine with church music, burgundy with tragic opera, champagne with comic opera, and punch with a highly romantic work like *Don Giovanni*." Hoffmann composed a dozen operas (his best known being *Undine*, produced in Berlin in 1816) but he is most familiar to music-lovers as the central figure of an opera himself, Jacques Offenbach's *The Tales of Hoffmann*.

Hoffmann, who was in his teens when Mozart died, adored him so much that he changed his third baptismal name, Wilhelm, to Amadeus, thus arriving at the initials E. T. A., by which he has become known to posterity. His stories are replete with musical allusions and incidents, and few are more gripping and mysterious than his "Don Juan" tale.

In this story a traveler in central Europe finds that his hotel room has an extra door that opens into a private loge in an adjacent opera house where *Don Giovanni* is about to be performed. He quickly enters the box, takes his seat, and listens to the Overture, which conjures up all sorts of vivid and disturbing images in his mind: "The seventh bar of the *allegro*, with its jubilant fanfare, became the voice of crime itself, exulting. Out of the dark night I saw demons stretch their fiery claws and loom menacingly over the lives of carefree mortals dancing merrily on the thin lid of a bottomless pit. . . ."

Absorbed in the action of the first act, the traveler suddenly becomes aware, through a scent of perfume and a rustle of skirts, that a woman has entered the box behind him. "Engrossed in the poetic world of the opera," he pays little attention, but when the act ends he turns around and to his astonishment finds that his companion is Donna Ana, the heroine of the work, herself.

Music is her only reality, the beautiful woman tells him, by way of explaining how she can simultaneously exist in his box and on the stage. The two hold a fascinating conversation in which the traveler realizes that she really is a kind of superwoman destined to do battle against Don Juan—the divine versus the demonic.

At the end of Hoffmann's tale the traveler retires to his room after the opera but, unable to sleep, consumes a bowl of punch and reenters the loge in the empty theater to muse upon his strange encounter and Mozart's music. As the clock strikes two A.M. he feels "a warm, electric breath" and the "caressing scent of Italian perfume," but this time there is no visitor. The next morning at the *table d'hôte* he hears that during the night the prima donna was taken suddenly ill and died, precisely at two A.M.

In this and many other tales, the romantic imagination seized upon certain of Mozart's works and made them its own. Nor has it ever really let go of them, even though the twentieth century has brought with it a broader and more comprehensive view.

The Shavian Mozart

"All of my musical self-respect is based on my keen appreciation of Mozart's works. It is as still true as it was before the Eroica Symphony *existed, that there is nothing better in art than Mozart's best."*

—George Bernard Shaw,
The World, April 19, 1893

Bernard Shaw is so well-known for his advocacy of the music of Richard Wagner in the 1890s that his efforts to sharpen his contemporaries' awareness of Mozart's true stature are often overlooked. Shaw was not only the perfect Wagnerite, he also was the ideal Mozartean, a listener capable of taking the full measure of the composer's genius.

Shaw's music criticism, written principally for two London journals, the *Star* and *The World*, from 1888 to 1894, was first published in book form in the 1930s; nevertheless its value and

215

significance even today are not entirely appreciated. For Shaw, despite such gaffes as his constant disparagement of Johannes Brahms (whom he despised as the antithesis of his favorite, Wagner), was a shrewd and sapient critic, far in advance of his fellow Victorians in his understanding of Mozart.

Much of Mozart's music was now available in England for playing or for studying, and Shaw seized the opportunity to do both. When he was a boy in Dublin his mother took singing lessons, and Bernard used to listen attentively during her instruction and practice sessions. In fact, he began to sing himself and had acquired a considerable repertory of arias and songs when Mrs. Shaw decided to move to London to pursue her musical work, leaving Bernard behind with his father. Shaw, then sixteen, found himself for the first time in a house without music and, to make his life more trying, his voice was beginning to change. "It was in vain now to sing," he afterward wrote. "My native woodnotes wild—just then breaking frightfully— could not satisfy my intense craving for the harmony which is the emotional substance of music and for the rhythmic figures of accompaniment which are its action and movement. I had only a single splintering voice and I wanted an orchestra."

So Shaw decided to learn the piano, his mother having thoughtfully neglected to sell the family instrument. Bernard sat himself down at the keyboard and "without troubling Czerny or Plaidy," whose exercises were then—and still are—standard for beginners, proceeded to arrange his fingers upon the keys for the opening chord of the Overture to *Don Giovanni*. It took ten minutes to do this, Shaw remembered, "but when it sounded right at last, it was worth all the trouble it cost."

Thus, with Mozart, began the musical career of George Bernard Shaw. He never became a professional pianist, though he did some accompanying after he moved to London, playing at gatherings of his friends. But he used his pianistic knowledge to explore musical literature by what he called "stumbling through" piano arrangements of symphonic and operatic pieces. He learned music through the best of all possible methods—playing it himself.

Shaw's musical knowledge saved his job when he was about to be fired as an editorial writer for the *Star* because of his radical political views; instead, he was made the paper's music critic. Since at the time his name was little known he adopted the pseudonym of Corno di Bassetto—not a titled foreigner, but a woodwind instrument that had become obsolete. Mozart had used it in his Requiem, one of the works Shaw had studied.

Even at this early stage of his career Shaw inveighed against the way that Mozart's music was performed in England. Until Hans Richter, the eminent German conductor, directed the Symphony No. 39 in E-flat in London in the 1880s, Shaw wrote, "nobody could have gathered . . . that Mozart, judged by nineteenth-century standards, had any serious claim to his old-fashioned reputation." And in speaking of Sir August Manns, another German, who had settled in London to become music director at the Crystal Palace, Shaw commented tartly: "A performance under Manns of a Mozart symphony was deplorably like two young ladies at Brixton playing a pianoforte duet. Mozart is the test: he is the master of masters."

Shaw also refused to accept the prevalent sentimentalized view of Mozart as a kind of musical nature boy. Writing in his weekly column in *The World* on December 9, 1891, on the occasion of the 100th anniversary of Mozart's death, he offered this remarkably clear-sighted appraisal of his place in musical history:

> The Mozart Centenary had made a great deal of literary and musical business this week. . . . The word is, of course, Admire, admire, admire; but unless you

frankly trade on the ignorance of the public, and cite as illustrations of his unique genius feats that come easily to dozens of organists and choir-boys who never wrote, and never will write, a bar of original music in their lives, or pay his symphonies empty compliments that might be transferred word for word, without the least incongruity, to the symphonies of Spohr and the operas of Offenbach; or represent him as composing as spontaneously as a bird sings, on the strength of his habit of perfecting his greater compositions in his mind before he wrote them down—unless you try these well-worn dodges, you will find nothing to admire that is peculiar to Mozart: the fact being that he, like Praxiteles, Raphael, Molière or Shakespear, was no leader of a new departure or founder of a school.

He came at the end of a development, not at the beginning of one; and although there are operas and symphonies, and even pianoforte sonatas and pages of instrumental scoring of his, on which you can put your finger and say, "Here is final perfection in this manner; and nobody, whatever his genius may be, will ever get a step further on these lines," you cannot say, "Here is an entirely new vein of musical art, of which nobody ever dreamt before Mozart." ... Many Mozart worshippers cannot bear to be told that their hero was not the founder of a dynasty. But in art the highest success is to be the last of your race, not the first. Anybody, almost, can make a beginning: the difficulty is to make an end—to do what cannot be bettered.

In his treatise on Wagner, *The Perfect Wagnerite*, Shaw described Mozart as a "a dramatist comparable to Molière." As a dramatist himself, Shaw, according to his biographer Archibald Henderson, is alleged to have felt flattered only once in his life, when the great scientist Albert Einstein told him that his works were like Mozart's notes—"every one of them meant something and was exactly in its proper place."

Mozartean echoes occur in a number of Shaw's dramatic writings, but nowhere as memorably as in his masterpiece of 1903, *Man and Superman*, his own version of the Don Juan story. Shaw patterns his characters upon those of the Mozart opera to the point of retaining their identities and in some cases their names. Thus, John Tanner, M.I.R.C. (Member of the Idle Rich Class), is Don Juan Tenorio; Ann Whitfield is Donna Ana; Octavius is Don Ottavio; and the Statue, of course, the Statue. Shaw is attempting far more than a modern parallel to the classic Don Juan story. His play, subtitled "A Comedy and a Philosophy," is an examination of human relations, notably those between men and women, and serves as a platform for the introduction of the Shavian Superman, the terrestrial tool of the Life Force that strives to make mankind ever better.

But, as with most Shaw plays, theatergoers and readers are likely to ignore the philosophy and enjoy the comedy, and in *Man and Superman* much of this takes the form of Mozartean echoes. These are especially evident in Act III, the famous "Don Juan in Hell" scene which is, to quote Shaw's own description, "a totally extraneous act in which my hero, enchanted by the air of the Sierra, has a dream in which his Mozartean ancestor appears and philosophizes at great length in a Shavio-Socratic dialogue with the lady, the statue and the devil."

Shaw's stage directions call for the scene to be introduced with music from *Don Giovanni*. When the Statue of the Commander is about to enter it is preceded by "two great chords rolling in on syncopated waves of sound . . . D minor and its dominant: a sound of dreadful joy to all musicians." The Devil later appears to the same chords, but "this time Mozart's music gets grotesquely adulterated with Gounod's." The Devil and the Statue later sing a convivial snatch of the Don's music, leading Juan to remark wryly that "Hell is full of musical amateurs: music is the brandy of the damned." Finally, the scene ends as the Statue and the Devil descend in a red glow down the operatic trapdoor of *Don Giovanni*, with the Commander remarking: "Ah, this reminds me of old times."

Performances of *Man and Superman* including "Don Juan in Hell" are infrequent, for they run to well over five hours. Occasionally the scene is given by itself, and it makes for a splendid evening's entertainment. Perhaps the most notable production was the 1952 production in New York with Charles Boyer as Don Juan, Charles Laughton as the Devil, Agnes Moorehead as Anna, and Cedric Hardwicke as the statue—a performance subsequently recorded by Columbia Records.

Shaw's *Man and Superman*, like Mozart's *Don Giovanni*, represents an artist operating at the peak of his powers; together they provide a shining instance of the stimulus that one great creative mind can give to another.

Mozart in America

I hear those odes, symphonies, operas;
I hear in the William Tell, *the music of an arous'd*
    and angry people;
I hear Meyerbeer's Huguenots, *the* Prophet, *or*
    Robert;
Gounod's Faust, *or Mozart's* Don Juan.

        —Walt Whitman, "Proud Music of the Storm,"
                Leaves of Grass, 1868

Throughout the nineteenth century, in America as elsewhere, Mozart was the victim of a sentimentalized
view taken both of his personality and his music. A hymn
collection published in Boston in 1849 almost turned him into
a Tiny Tim or a Little Eva in a fanciful account it gave of his
last days. In this touching little tale, as Mozart is about to breathe

his last he finishes the Requiem (which he never did), bids farewell to his daughter Emilie (who never existed), and prepares contentedly to ascend to heaven and meet his wife (who outlived him by fifty years). So outlandish is this narrative that a composer named James Willey actually turned it into a satirical stage work called *The Death of Mozart* in 1976.

Even more important than the distortion of Mozart's character in early America was the neglect of his music, which received only occasional performances and then only of a handful of works. When the Philharmonic Society of New York came into being on December 7, 1842, its first program included Beethoven's Fifth Symphony, Weber's Overture to *Oberon*, another overture by Johann Wenzell Kalliwoda, and several shorter pieces, including one aria by Mozart, from *The Abduction from the Seraglio*. Even when Theodore Thomas organized his famous traveling orchestra specializing in Germanic repertory it was Beethoven who dominated the programs, with only a minor role allocated to Mozart. Performances by other orchestras were intermittent at best: the *Jupiter* Symphony was played by the Philharmonic Society in 1844 and again in 1847; the G minor Symphony by the Musical Fund Society of Boston in 1850, and the Requiem by the Handel and Haydn Society of Boston in 1857. In 1847 a Mozart Society was organized in Chicago.

Operatically the situation was only marginally better. Walt Whitman, who loved opera and attended performances whenever he could (often, when he was a newspaper man in Brooklyn, on free tickets), enumerated in his poetry and prose the titles of twenty-five different operas he heard at such locales as Niblo's Gardens in Manhattan. Only one of these, *Don Giovanni*, was by Mozart. In America, as in England, this was the only truly popular Mozart opera for many years. By contrast, *The Marriage of Figaro*, though given in an adaptation by Henry Bishop in New York in 1823, was seldom heard during subsequent decades.

The *Magic Flute*, however, was presented a bit more frequently. One performance, at Grover's Theater in Washington, D.C., on March 15, 1865, was attended by no less a personage than the president of the United States, Abraham Lincoln, who occupied a box with Mrs. Lincoln and a few friends. Mrs. Lincoln, bored, wanted to leave before the end, but the president replied: "Oh, no, I want to see it out." Then, apparently feeling that a further amplication was required, he added: "It's best when you undertake a job to finish it." One month later Lincoln was assassinated while seated in a box at Ford's Theater.

Don Giovanni was among the works performed in the very first season of the Metropolitan Opera in New York in 1883, but for many years thereafter was given only sporadically. *The Marriage of Figaro* had its premiere ten years later but was performed very infrequently and was dropped completely from the repertory from 1917 to 1939—a twenty-two-year banishment. *The Magic Flute* had five presentations in 1899 in an Italian translation as *Il flauto magico* rather than as the authentically German *Die Zauberflöte*, but it also went unperformed for decades at a time. To carry the record further, America's leading opera house didn't attempt *Così fan tutte* until 1921, *The Abduction from the Seraglio* until 1946, *Idomeneo* until 1982, and *La Clemenza di Tito* until 1984. *Don Giovanni* remains the most frequently given of all Mozart operas at the Metropolitan, ranking nineteenth on its all-time list (as of 1985), but both *The Magic Flute* and *The Marriage of Figaro*, particularly the latter, have been gaining on it in recent years.

Only in the middle of the twentieth century did a general upsurge of appreciation for and understanding of Mozart really become apparent. Not until 1932 did an American, Marcia Davenport, produce an authoritative biography of Mozart (it still is in print). As late as 1938, Oscar Thompson, the music critic of the *New York Sun*, was writing that "it is obvious that a Mozart public must be developed comparable to that of the Wagner or Verdi public"; and in 1941 writer Cecil Smith observed in the *Chicago Tribune* that "the conception of Mozart as a composer of completely regular, four-square, boxlike musical structures has unhappily gained almost universal currency."

Yet within a period of fifteen or twenty years, this same music attained a remarkable popularity and ascendancy in American musical life. A survey of twenty-seven leading American orchestras revealed that while in the 1890–95 period Mozart ranked tenth in frequency of performance, by 1965–70 he had risen to third place, surpassed only by Beethoven and Brahms. Even more impressive was another survey conducted in the late 1960s by Broadcast Music, Inc. This extended to a broad spectrum of 417 orchestras in the United States and Canada, including college and community groups, with the results listing the ten most frequently performed composers, in order, as Mozart, Beethoven, Tchaikovsky, Brahms, Wagner, Haydn, Bach, Stravinsky, Ravel, and Mendelssohn.

What is the explanation for this remarkable turnaround? The growth of musical literacy in the country undoubtedly was one reason, but other factors were operating as well. For one thing, musicians themselves began paying greater attention to this enormous treasury of neglected music. Sir Thomas Beecham's recordings, along with those of the Glyndebourne Opera, circulated widely among American music lovers. Other conductors began to play more and more Mozart, with some of them, including such sensitive performers as Bruno Walter, George Szell, Fritz Stiedry, Fritz Reiner, Erich Leinsdorf, and Julius Rudel, being part of the exodus of talented musicians to the United States from Adolf Hitler's Europe.

Outside of the concert hall, radio broadcasts made Mozart's music available to thousands. The first complete cycle of Mozart piano concertos was given not in a hall but over New York radio station WOR. The advent of long-playing records contributed to the boom; in an almost uncanny way, the Mozart symphonies all seemed to fit very comfortably onto one side of an LP. Even television made an important contribution, with the now-vanished NBC Opera Theater producing English-language versions of *The Magic Flute* in 1956 and *Don Giovanni* in 1960, the latter with a cast that included Cesare Siepi and the young Leontyne Price. Mozart was also taken up by choreographers, most notably by George Balanchine in his *Symphonie Concertante* in 1947 and *Divertimento No. 15* in 1956.

In many ways, Mozart has become a kind of special-occasion composer, with Mozart festivals, Mozart weekends, Mozart marathons, and the like becoming almost a commonplace in many parts of the country. When the full-scale Tanglewood Festival at Lenox, Massachusetts, had to be abandoned because of travel restrictions during World War II, Serge Koussevitzky replaced it with a Mozart mini-festival. Tanglewood also became the site for the first performance ever given in the United States of the opera *Idomeneo*, conducted in 1947 by Boris Goldovsky. At the Solemn Pontifical Mass in Boston for the slain president John F. Kennedy, it was the Mozart Requiem that was performed. The bicentennial year of Mozart's birth, 1956, saw a tremendous outpouring of recordings, concerts, celebrations, and publications, and the flow has never slackened since.

Underlying all these manifestations, of course, has been a tremendous public avidity for Mozart's music. Twentieth-century taste seems more attuned to his style than was that of any previous era, including his own. Ludwig van Beethoven and Richard Wagner could disparage an opera like *Così fan tutte* as immoral, but modern audiences have no problem with its cynical, ironic story of two young men who test their love by switching partners.* As a result some of Mozart's most subtle and beautiful music has been restored to life after more than a century of neglect and misunderstanding. Mozart's operas, with their emphasis on ensemble and acting, have accorded admirably with the values of American singers and audiences alike. And they are readily translatable—no operatic composer is performed as frequently in English in the United States as Mozart.

The predilection for Mozart has also been reflected in some unexpected areas of American life. In 1969 researchers at Texas Tech University in Lubbock conducted some experiments in animal psychology involving the testing of newborn albino rats. The announced scientific objective was to determine whether animals that seldom make noise themselves could respond to the arranged sound that human beings know as music. To this end, one set of rats were made to listen to Mozart selections including portions of the Symphonies Nos. 40 and 41 and the Violin Concerto in A, while a second group were played a series of modern selections including Arnold Schönberg's *Pierrot lunaire* and *Transfigured Night*. Then, after a two-week respite from any sounds at all, the rats were permitted to opt, by entering the appropriate cage, for the sounds they preferred. Overwhelmingly, they selected Mozart.

The results of the experiment may be a bit murky scientifically, and they don't prove very much about music, either. But how else would you really have expected the rats to vote?

---

*Wagner's fatuous comment was: "O how doubly dear and above all honor is Mozart to me, that it was not possible for him to invent music for *Tito* like that of *Don Giovanni*, for *Così fan tutte* like that of *Figaro*! How shamefully it would have desecrated music!"

How Mozart Became Mostly

"Our emphasis isn't on big-name soloists; it's on the music—meaning mostly on Mozart—and on performers who know how to play it."

—William W. Lockwood, Jr., 1979

In many ways, the most significant of all Mozart festivals is one of the newest, the Mostly Mozart Festival of New York. Originating in Lincoln Center in 1966, it has prospered and expanded from the start, has traveled to other cities and towns, and has been imitated widely in the United States and abroad.

Unlike the older European festivals, Mostly Mozart is a popularly oriented event, with comparatively low prices and a complete lack of social trimmings. Furthermore, while the European festivals concentrate upon Mozart's operas, Mostly

Mozart covers an enormous spectrum of his music, with the operas perhaps the least well represented. In its first twenty years, Mostly Mozart has performed over two-thirds of all of Mozart's compositions, from K. 1 to K. 626. No other musical event anywhere at any time has offered as comprehensive a view of his music.

Mostly Mozart came into being because Lincoln Center for the Performing Arts, then a brand-new cultural center on New York's West Side, needed an event to fill Philharmonic Hall (later renamed Avery Fisher Hall) during the summer months, when it otherwise would have remained dark. Summer festivals are usually rural or at least rustic in setting, rather than urban; at the very least they are staged in city parks or other leafy places. For years New York City offered one major summer event, the Lewisohn Stadium Concerts held on the concrete tiers of the City College athletic field, at which Mozart was reasonably well represented, but this went out of existence when the stadium was torn down.

Lincoln Center didn't consciously set out to replace the Stadium Concerts, but it did feel that good music would attract large numbers of young New Yorkers during the summer. Accordingly a team of enterprising concert managers, Jay K. Hoffman and George Schutz, were engaged in 1966 to organize a suitable concert series. It was decided to run for one month, charge a top price of $3, and play music only by Mozart. The series was called Mid-Summer Serenades: A Mozart Festival. "None of it could have happened without the direct help of William Schuman, who then was the president of Lincoln Center," Jay Hoffman recalls. "His only condition was that we engage New York musicians for the orchestra."

Astonishingly, the concerts were an instant success, with the twenty-six programs attracting 54,000 paying customers, amounting to 76 percent of Philharmonic Hall's capacity. That first season more than 100 orchestral, chamber, and solo pieces were performed. In a brief article expressing surprise at the audience response, *Time* magazine commented: "Skeptics would have considered Mozart box-office suicide during a dreary New York summer."

After two years the Lincoln Center authorities decided to take over the summer concerts themselves, and Hoffman and Schutz departed, not without a certain amount of feeling on both sides. William W. Lockwood of the Lincoln Center administration became festival director, the season was lengthened, and the programs were broadened to include other composers such as Haydn, Beethoven, and Schubert. "The idea was," says Lockwood, "to also play music by composers either who influenced Mozart or were influenced by him." In 1971 the series was called Mostly Mozart for the first time. "I take credit for that," says Lockwood. "Since we were playing mostly Mozart I said let's call it that."

The name Mostly Mozart caught on immediately. In fact, it became such a catchword that the festival began to use it as a marketing tool, with the imprint decorating T-shirts, mugs, duffel bags, sun visors, note paper, pens, neckties, and dozens of other souvenir articles. The name is now copyrighted, but since there can be no legal restrictions on its use abroad, Mostly Mozart concerts now exist at such distant locales as the Barbican Center in London and in Sydney, Australia.

Although Mostly Mozart has the reputation for attracting youthful audiences, the actual figures compiled by the administration indicate that it also draws substantially from among middle-aged and older concertgoers. According to the Lincoln Center demographics, 23 percent of Mostly Mozart ticket-buyers are under the age of thirty-four, 20 percent are from thirty-five to forty-four, 40 percent from forty-five to sixty-four, and 17 percent over sixty-four. Half are from Manhattan, but there is good representation from suburban areas and a sprinkling of out-of-towners. Eighty percent are returnees from previous seasons, and in any given summer 50 percent attend more than two concerts and 30 percent five or more. Obviously Mostly Mozart is habit-forming.

By 1985 the Mostly Mozart season had lengthened to seven weeks and was selling around 115,000 tickets a summer, running to an average of 85-percent capacity (Avery Fisher Hall has 2,736 seats). Prices had risen to a top price of $13, with coupon books available for $10 a seat. "It's still a cheap date if you're into music," Lockwood contends.

The Mostly Mozart orchestra is now a permanent organization rather than the shifting assemblage of free-lancers of its early days. Since 1984 Gerard Schwarz has had the title of Music Director, with a contract extending through 1987. Since 1981, the festival has traveled to Washington, D.C., for a series at the John F. Kennedy Center for the Performing Arts, and it also plays single-night concerts in the New York area. Under the sponsorship of the New York Telephone Company, the festival has launched a three-year series of spring or autumn appearances in upstate New York cities including Schenectady, Ithaca, Potsdam and Poughkeepsie, not to mention Brooklyn, Queens, and Staten Island.

Why has Mostly Mozart been so successful? William Lockwood believes one of the reasons is that Mozart's music, for all its rise in popularity, is still too little played in the standard concert hall. "If you look at the programs of many orchestras during the 1970s you'll find relatively little Mozart scheduled," he says. "Many orchestras and conductors feel that Mozart doesn't show them off. There also are some concertgoers who have the impression that with only a small complement of players on the stage to play a Mozart symphony they're somehow being cheated of full value. We have demonstrated, among other things, that Mozart is proven box-office, and I think we have influenced other orchestras to program more Mozart."

Strictly from the musical standpoint, Mostly Mozart has revealed the breadth and variety of Mozart's artistic achievement as no other festival has ever attempted to do. The festival seeks to find a balance between the better-known works that listeners look forward to with anticipation, and more obscure but no less worthy compositions.

"Every year we try to add a few pieces that we've never played before," Lockwood says. "We even try to put on at least one work a season that is *never* done. We have given a lot of terrific Mozart that nobody ever gives. In 1983 we did the opera *Zaide*, in 1985 *Mitridate, rè di Ponto*.

"We have performed all of Mozart's symphonies, all of his piano concertos including the childhood ones, all of his violin concertos including the one he didn't write, all of the string quartets and quintets. The most popular works, the ones we've given most, are the last three symphonies, Nos. 39, 40 and 41. The Clarinet Quintet has become a particular favorite—it is kind of our equivalent of the *Trout* Quintet."

Then with a laugh Bill Lockwood adds: "Sometimes I have a dream. Mozart appears to me and asks whether I'd like him to write some more music, and I answer: 'Well, if it wouldn't be too much trouble, we could use a few more piano quartets and maybe a viola or a cello concerto.' "

Lockwood notes with considerable pride that Mostly Mozart nowadays is attracting a full share of "name" players, all of them distinguished not only by their reputations but by their adeptness in the Mozart repertory. In 1985 alone the roster included sopranos Elly Ameling, Erie Mills, Edith Mathis, and Arleen Auger; pianists Horacio Gutierrez, Garrick Ohlsson, André Watts, Emanuel Ax, and Claudio Arrau; flutist Jean-Pierre Rampal; clarinetist Richard Stoltzman; and trumpeter Wynton Marsalis. Appearing three times was the great Spanish pianist Alicia de Laroccha, who is there almost every year and has become the uncrowned queen of Mostly Mozart.

"When we started out," Lockwood recalls, "we almost had to beg performers to appear. They were very dubious. 'What is it?' they wanted to know. 'What kind of concerts did you say?' How different it has become! Now they're all clamoring to play Mozart."

Mozart at the Movies

"Nobody has suffered more than Mozart from sentimental misjudgment."

—Peter Shaffer,
The New York Times, September 2, 1984

The greatest recent impetus to the popularity of Mozart has undoubtedly come from the motion picture *Amadeus*, directed by Milos Forman and based on Peter Shaffer's play of the same name. The film version of *Amadeus* won eight Academy Awards, played in hundreds of movie houses, acquainted millions of people for the first time with both the man and his music.

Mozart has not been a complete stranger to cinematic treatment, for a number of efforts have been made to produce documentaries about his life, usually in the German language.

At least three such examples, Karl Hartl's *The Life and Loves of Mozart* (1959), Hans Conrad Fischer's *The Life of Mozart* (1966), and Klaus Kirchner's *Mozart: A Childhood Chronicle* (1976), were exported to America but failed to find a substantial audience. Prior to *Amadeus*, Mozart's most notable movie involvement came in the romantic Swedish film *Elvira Madigan* (1965), in which the Andante movement of his Piano Concerto No. 21 in C was utilized extensively for the soundtrack. Such was the effectiveness of the score that the concerto was promptly subtitled "*Elvira Madigan*" in some concert listings, including those of the Mostly Mozart Festival. A recording by the pianist Geza Anda, who played the music heard in the movie, reached the best-seller list when it was marketed with a sticker reading: "Contains Theme from Elvira Madigan."

In the 1970s attempts began to be made to produce film versions of Mozart's operas. Ingmar Bergman's *The Magic Flute* (1975) added some beautifully imaginative cinematic touches to Mozart and Schikaneder's stage piece. The Swedish director not only conveyed the fantasy, humor, and spirituality of the work; he embellished it with such additions as flavorsome glimpses of the characters offstage—carefree Papageno almost sleeping through his entrance cue; the Queen of the Night brazenly puffing a cigarette under a No Smoking sign; the scholarly Sarastro studying the score of his next opera, which happens to be *Parsifal*; the noble couple, Tamino and Pamina, playing chess together. Even though it was sung in Swedish mainly by singers of local renown, Bergman's *The Magic Flute* had a nobility and enchantment of its own, and it continues to undergo periodic revival.

Considerably more prosaic was Joseph Losey's *Don Giovanni* (1979), in which the action was constrained by being filmed almost entirely in a villa near Vicenza in northern Italy. The performers were largely lacking in visual charm and attractiveness, and the direction for the most part was leaden and literal. Losey's *Don Giovanni* was dependent almost entirely upon its musical virtues, which were substantial, but it did little to advance the cause of opera as a cinematic art.

With such a spotty record, there was little reason to anticipate the tremendous success of *Amadeus* among moviegoers, especially considering that the play had been something of an intellectual exercise. Although the play, staged first in London in 1979 and transplanted to Broadway in 1981, bore Mozart's name in the title, it really was built around his rival Salieri. Shaffer, already the author of such admired dramas as *The Royal Hunt of the Sun* and *Equus*, was fascinated by the artistic and personal contrasts he saw embodied in the two composers. He envisioned Salieri as a pious, hard-working, dedicated journeyman and Mozart as a crude, silly, irresponsible genius. Lacking the divine gift, Salieri knows he is condemned to mediocrity; and he is galled beyond measure that such supreme creative powers have been bestowed instead upon a foolish boy. It is this injustice, and not mere envy, that embitters Salieri against God and resolves him to plot his rival's demise.

Actually this is by no means a novel theme, for the British playwright was anticipated more than a century earlier by the great Russian poet Alexander Pushkin in the dramatic episode *Mozart and Salieri*, later turned into an opera by Nikolai Rimsky-Korsakov. In Pushkin's little drama, as in Shaffer's play, the theme is stated by Salieri at the outset:

> *Men say: there is no justice upon earth.*
> *But neither is there justice in the Heavens!. . .*
> *Where, where is justice, when the sacred gift*
> *Of deathless genius comes not to reward*
> *Impassioned love and utter self-denial,*

> *And toil and striving and beseeching prayer,*
> *But puts her halo round a lack-wit's skull,*
> *A frivolous idler's brow? . . . O Mozart, Mozart!*

The Mozart depicted by Pushkin, like that of Shaffer, is flighty, giggling, and impetuous; when he meets a blind street fiddler giving a wretched performance of his aria *"Voi che sapete"* he delightedly drags him along to play for Salieri—who is scandalized that Mozart can listen to such a poor rendition of his own music.

Pushkin's Salieri also is painfully aware of the inferiority of his own talent, but justifies his decision to poison Mozart by a desire to clear the way not merely for himself, but for all composers to follow:

> *If he lives on, then all of us will perish—*
> *High priests and servants of the art of music—*
> *Not I alone with my o'ershadowed glory.*
> *And what will it avail if Mozart live*
> *And scale still higher summits of perfection?*
> *Will he thereby raise art itself? No, no,*
> *'Twill fall again when once he disappears.*

So he hands Mozart the poisoned cup. Raising it, Mozart says:

> *I drink, and pledge that sacred covenant*
> *That links the names of Mozart and Salieri,*
> *Two sons of harmony. . . .*

Peter Shaffer's play is at once more complex and superficial than Pushkin's. It is complex in that it involves an array of secondary characters including Constanze, Baron van Swieten,

Emperor Joseph II, and others, but superficial in its almost total failure to probe Mozart's mind and character. Shaffer ignores the brilliant discussions about music and about life in Mozart's correspondence with his father; but he seizes on the scatological passages in the letters and transfers them to his everyday speech. There even are hints in the play of a sadomasochistic relationship between Mozart and his wife. Mozart is made out to be a total boob, a thoroughly crude and vulgar boy, redeemed only by his ability to compose great music—which in the play must be taken on faith, since there is very little of it to be heard, and that only by means of the theater's tinny sound system.

But Mozart actually is only a secondary figure; the play really belongs to Salieri, who is depicted as a cultivated, personable, and courtly figure, sensitive enough to recognize the artistic chasm that separates Mozart from himself and human enough to agonize over it. Salieri opens and closes the play with lengthy monologues and dominates its development with continuing explanations of his thoughts, feelings, emotions, and actions. At times it almost seems that instead of poisoning Mozart he is trying to talk him to death.

In the course of Amadeus's transfer from the stage to the screen, a great many things happened both to the story and to the characters. Where the play is stylized, wordy, and abstract, the movie is natural, action-filled, and human. Salieri still provides the motivation and the rationale, but Mozart now becomes a worthy antagonist as a person no less than as a musician. His life and his feelings are depicted more fully, so that he ceases to be a mere illustration of Salieri's thesis of divine injustice and is shown as a human being with his own needs and problems. Especially in the latter part of the movie it is Mozart who dominates and who, through his decline and death, engages the viewer's sympathy and concern.

Unfortunately, this change in approach is achieved at a

Left: The romanticized Mozart painted by his brother-in-law Joseph Lange. *Right:* The cinematic Mozart depicted by Tom Hulce in *Amadeus*.

price—an even greater falsification of historical events than that of the stage version. An extensive list could be drawn up of the distortions and omissions that disfigure the movie, but a few of the more obvious may suffice:

- While the movie shows the dying Mozart dictating his Requiem to Salieri, it actually was his pupil and assistant Süssmayr who helped him with it and finally completed the score. Süssmayr's existence is nowhere mentioned in the movie. Neither, for that matter, is that of Lorenzo da Ponte, who played a far more critical role in Mozart's life than many of the characters who are shown in the film.

- Constanze Mozart may have been prone to spending time at the spa in Baden, but she never packed up and ran out on her husband, as she is made to do in the movie. Nor did she ever throw Mozart's father out of their house.

- Mozart enjoyed his wine, but there is no report of his having been seen drunk in public or guzzling a bottle during a performance.

- Salieri never planted a servant girl in the Mozart household as a spy, nor was it he who commissioned Mozart to compose the Requiem.

- Neither Mozart nor Salieri ever conducted an entire performance with two hands—late-eighteenth-century practice generally was to conduct from the keyboard. This is one of a number of stylistic gaffes in the movie.

Of course such errors and exaggerations result not from ignorance on the part of the filmmakers but from what they regard as cinematic and dramatic necessity. Shaffer himself is well versed in music; for a few years in the early 1960s he was a music critic for the British publication *Time and Tide*. Milos Forman, the Czech-born director, acknowledges that he knew very little about Mozart's life and was acquainted with only his most popular works, but says he found himself "hooked" on the story of Shaffer's play which he regarded as "magnificently theatrical." He and Shaffer worked for five months taking the play apart and putting it together again, adding such characters as Leopold Mozart, Schikaneder, and various courtiers, and devising the new ending in which Salieri almost demonically forces the exhausted Mozart to dictate to him the music of the Requiem until he falls back dead.

Such scenes, Shaffer wrote afterward, are "obviously indefensible on factual grounds but, I hope, just as obviously defensible on those theatrical and cinematic ones which must always take precedence in a work of dramatic fiction." *Amadeus*, he went on to argue, is not a screen biography but "a fantasia on events in Mozart's life." Upon the movie, he added, "I invoke the blessing of Mozart himself—solely as a man of the theater. For that, supremely, was what he was."

Whatever opinion Mozart's shade may hold, many of his earthly admirers were outraged by Shaffer's approach and treatment. Even the play, when originally produced in London, had its share of detractors; among the adjectives applied to it by dissenting critics were "appalling," "inflated," and "sentimental." But such negative comments seem almost trifling in the face of the indignation expressed by a number of American music-lovers who denounced both the movie's historical inaccuracies and its portrayal of Mozart's personal characteristics. One veteran musician, Dr. Maurice Zam, former director of the Los Angeles Conservatory of Music, actually mailed out copies of a printed broadside entitled "Why I Abhor *Amadeus*," beginning: "Warning: *Amadeus* is dangerous to your musical health. It may prevent you from appreciating Mozart's music, and pervert and poison your capacity for intelligent listening to all kinds of music."

Perhaps the most positive element of *Amadeus*—and one frequently overlooked by moviegoers and critics—is its adroit and intelligent use of Mozart's music. The relative absence of music was one of the deficiencies of the play; the movie soundtrack, on the other hand, is made up of works by Mozart and his contemporaries that, by the reality of their presence, consistently illustrate and underline the drama. Thus the turbulent strains of the Symphony No. 25 in G minor, K. 183, open the movie on a dramatically passionate note, and the Romanza of his D minor Piano Concerto, K. 466, brings it to a close with a kind of benediction as the credits are shown.

Substantial excerpts from other works are also heard, all of them in first-class performances directed by Neville Marriner with the accomplished musicians of the Academy of St. Martin's-in-the-Fields in London. Not least impressive are portions of several Mozart operas including the supper scene of *Don Giovanni*. The operatic scenes, like much of the dramatic action, were filmed in Prague; and the stage used was that of the Tyl Theater, where *Don Giovanni* actually had its premiere in 1787. Even Salieri gets his musical due, for included in the movie is a generous section of perhaps his most distinguished work, the opera *Axur*—probably the only presentation it has had in any form for at least a hundred years.

To at least one music-lover, *Amadeus* is a memorable movie-going experience. Its recreation of the physical surroundings and artistic atmosphere of the late eighteenth-century world is realistic and convincing. Some of its characters are drawn with extraordinary fidelity to the originals (Joseph II, for one, bears a striking physical likeness to his portraits, and Schikaneder's circusy musical troupe seems not very far from the mark). Most important of all, Mozart's music, set forth without alteration or adulteration, plays so central a role that it almost becomes a living character in the drama.

From the plays of Shakespeare to the operas of Verdi, historical authenticity has never been the ultimate measure of a work of art. *Amadeus* has its share of flaws and falsehoods, but this is not the first time in the annals of music that a dubious text has been redeemed by a glorious score.

Mozart Tomorrow

We who know little—which is just as well—
About the future can, at least, foretell,
Whether they live in air-borne nylon cubes,
Practice group-marriage or are fed through tubes,
That crowds two centuries from now, will press
(Absurd their hair, ridiculous their dress),
And pay in currencies however weird
To hear Sarastro booming through his beard....

—W. H. Auden,
"Metalogue to The Magic Flute," 1956

ust before the turn of the twentieth century the pianist and conductor Hans von Bülow remarked that Mozart was "a young man with a great future before him." It isn't clear whether von Bülow was bemoaning Mozart's premature death, or predicting that not until later generations would he be fully appreciated.

There is validity in both interpretations, though perhaps more in the second than in the first. How much more music Mozart might have written is among the most tantalizing questions in all art. His creative impulse showed no slackening; despite the misfortunes that overwhelmed him he kept on working and creating uncomplainingly. The last year of his life produced some of his most imperishable masterpieces.

What Mozart might have produced in a more normal life span—had he lived, let us say, to the age of sixty—is unimaginable. In all likelihood such works would have differed considerably from those by which we know him. Mozart composed in no rigid style; he was responsive to the artistic currents around him; he never stopped developing. Following his encounter with the music of Bach at Baron van Swieten's a new contrapuntal texture became apparent in his music. Had he lived into the age of Beethoven, who knows how the romantic and dramatic impulses already apparent in so many of his works might have deepened and broadened?

Yet, listening to the enormous body of music created by Mozart in his brief lifetime, no one feels cheated or deprived. His musical life, unlike that of Schubert, who died even younger, somehow seems fulfilled and complete. Works like the B-flat Piano Concerto, *The Magic Flute*, and the Requiem would provide a fitting climax for any career.

In the hundred years that have passed since von Bülow's pronouncement, his forecast that Mozart's music would find its public has been amply borne out. An entire industry has grown up around the composer and his music. Musicologists have sought out neglected works. Conductors have explored the fur-

thest reaches of his instrumental music. String quartets, wind
ensembles, all sorts of odd and unlikely combinations of instruments, have taken up with zest the pieces he left for them.
Vocalists have developed a whole new specialty of Mozart singing. Stage directors have attempted new approaches to his operas. "Original instrument" specialists have played his music on
reconstructed fortepianos; traditional performers have found it -
perfectly suited to modern keyboards. Critics have dissected his
scores; analysts probed his psyche; novelists revamped his life.

Mozart societies have come into being all over the world.
About seventy are included in a listing issued by the Mozarteum
in Salzburg. Among the countries represented are Argentina,
Australia, Austria, Brazil, Canada, Czechoslovakia, France, Ger-
many, Greenland, Hungary, Japan, the Netherlands, Spain,
Switzerland, and the United States. At last count, the United
States had Mozart societies of various sizes in Atlanta, Detroit,
Miami, New York, and Sea Island, Georgia, with a Canadian
group in Toronto.

Largest of these is the Friends of Mozart of New York,
which actually has a national membership. Established by Erna
Schwerin, a clinical psychologist, in 1975, it presents concerts
emphasizing rarely encountered works, sponsors lectures, issues
a regular newsletter, publishes monographs, and serves as a
clearinghouse for Mozart information. Another well-established
organization is the Japan Mozart Society, founded in Tokyo in
1955, which limits its membership to the magical Köchel number
of 626, and has a long waiting list of applicants.

What more can tomorrow add to the understanding and
appreciation of Mozart? Very little, perhaps; yet there is no
doubt that the process will go on. Some fifty works believed to
have been written by Mozart have never been found. Little
pieces keep turning up; in 1985, for instance, an early Symphony

in A minor, written at the age of nine, was discovered in Denmark, and received a cable-television performance as well as a U.S. concert premiere at Mostly Mozart. (Most authorities regard only its second movement as authentic; the rest is classified as "attributed.") Stage directors have by no means exhausted the possibilities of extravagant operatic productions; some of the more fantastic efforts of recent seasons have included a *Marriage of Figaro* played against a background of enlarged Boucher nudes, a *Così fan tutte* set in a neon-lit coffee-house complete to a functioning jukebox, and a *Magic Flute* in which Sarastro roamed the Temple of Wisdom clad in a business suit and sang his great aria about human brotherhood seated on Pamina's bed. Possibly there are a few more minor works still left to be recorded, although it is difficult to think of a "K number" that has been overlooked by the record companies, large or small. Finally, there is the suggestion made—how seriously one cannot say—by *London Times* columnist Bernard Levin, that Mozart be canonized as a saint, on the grounds that in a short span of time he worked "upwards of 600 miracles" besides having led a thoroughly moral, upright, and beneficent life.

So there may still be a few things left to be done. Mozart's story is never-ending; every century views him through its own eyes. To the eighteenth he was a dazzling virtuoso, to the nineteenth a painter of miniatures, to the twentieth a supreme musical dramatist. Surely the twenty-first will have its own evaluation to add. Yet it seems inconceivable that human esteem for Mozart and his music will ever diminish, for no career illustrates better than his the ancient truth that life is brief and art enduring.

APPENDIXES

A Mozart Chronology

Year (Age)	What He Did	What He Wrote
1756	Born January 27 at Salzburg.	
1759 (3)	Plays chords on clavier.	
1760 (4)	Starts lessons with father.	
1761 (5)	Composes little pieces.	
1762 (6)	Taken with his sister to Munich and Vienna by his father in his first appearances as a prodigy.	First keyboard pieces—four minuets and an allegro—listed in the Köchel catalogue (K. 1–5).
1763 (7)	Concert tour of Germany, Low Countries, and France with his father and sister.	First pieces for violin (K. 6–8), which he is able to play himself.

1764 (8)	Tour continues, with a prolonged stay in London during which he meets Johann Christian Bach and plays for King George III.	First symphonies (K. 16 and 19).
1765 (9)	Still in London until the autumn, followed by return to the Continent via The Hague, where he and Nannerl fall ill.	Another symphony (K. 22).
1766 (10)	More European concerts, including Versailles, Geneva, Munich. Return to Salzburg at year's end—the tour has lasted three and a half years!	Further works for piano and violin; begins getting commissions and dedicating works to royal patrons.
1767 (11)	A year mostly at home during which he and his sister overcome bouts with smallpox.	First piano concertos, adapted from works by others (K. 37, 39, 41); Latin comedy *Apollo and Hyacinthus*.
1768 (12)	Trips to Brno and Vienna, where he is received and given a watch by Maria Theresa.	Operas *La finta semplice* and *Bastien and Bastienne*.
1769 (13)	Begins trip to Italy with his father; makes a sensation in Verona.	Early masses and symphonies.

1770 (14)   Entire year in Italy, including Milan, Bologna, Florence, Naples, and Rome, where he copies Allegri's *Miserere*. Receives Order of the Golden Spur, meets Padre Martini.

First string quartet (K. 80); opera *Mitridate* produced in Milan, where it gets twenty-one performances.

1771 (15)   Returns to Salzburg for three months only to depart again for Italy for a six-month stay.

Opera *Ascanio in Alba*; more symphonies.

1772 (16)   Back in Salzburg where Hieronymus von Colloredo—his future foe—becomes archbishop. Third trip to Italy in the fall.

Writes stage piece *Il Sogno di Scipione* for Colloredo's accession; opera *Lucio Silla* and many other works.

1773 (17)   Attempts unsuccessfully to get a court appointment from Maria Theresa.

String quartets, divertimenti, motet *"Exsultate, jubilate."*

1774 (18)   At home until trip to Munich in December.

Mass in F (K. 192), Symphonies K. 199–202; opera *La finta giardiniera*; bassoon concerto.

1775 (19)   Most of the year in Salzburg.

Opera *Il Rè pastore*; five violin concertos.

1776 (20)	At home; deteriorating relations with Colloredo. *American Declaration of Independence*.	Many compositions including *Serenata notturna* (K. 239), *Haffner* Serenade (K. 250), and Concerto for Three Pianos (K. 242).
1777 (21)	Leaves with mother for projected visit to Paris; falls in love with sixteen-year-old Aloysia Weber on stopover in Mannheim.	Piano Concerto No. 9 in E-flat (K. 271), a new level of achievement for him.
1778 (22)	Prodded by his father, heads reluctantly for Paris, where his mother sickens and dies. En route home he visits Aloysia in Munich, but she rejects him.	"Parisian" works: Sinfonia Concertante for Winds, Concerto for Flute and Harp, Ballet *Les Petits Riens,* *Paris* Symphony (No. 31 in D, K. 297).
1779 (23)	Back to Salzburg, unhappily; takes job as Colloredo's court organist.	Sinfonia Concertante for Violin and Viola, another early masterpiece.

1780 (24)   In Salzburg until the end of the year, when he goes to Munich to prepare for *Idomeneo*. Writes incidental music to drama *Thamos, King of Egypt*, for Emanuel Schikaneder, later to be the librettist of *The Magic Flute*.

Idomeneo, Mass in C (K. 317).

1781 (25)   Resigns from Colloredo's service, heads for Vienna. Becomes engaged to Constanze Weber, Aloysia's younger sister. Has contest with Clementi. Meets Joseph Haydn—an eventful year!

Idomeneo performed. Oboe quartet (K. 370). Works on *The Abduction from the Seraglio*.

1782 (26)   Gives first big Vienna concert. Marries Constanze. *Abduction* is a hit in Vienna and is performed elsewhere as well.

Haffner Symphony (K. 385); Wind Serenade (K. 388); Piano Concertos (K. 413–415); String Quartet No. 14 (K. 387), first of the Haydn set.

1783 (27)   First son is born and dies. Wolfgang brings his wife to Salzburg to meet his father and sister, but no rapport is established.

Unfinished Mass in C minor (K. 427); *Linz* Symphony (No. 36, K. 425); another quartet (K. 428) for Haydn set.

1784 (28)	Son Karl Thomas is born. Mozart becomes deeply involved in Vienna's musical life. Joins the Freemasons. This is the start of his peak years as a composer.	Composes piano concertos for his own use (K. 449, 450, 451, 453, 459); Serenade for Thirteen Wind Instruments (K. 361); Quintet for Piano and Winds (K. 452).
1785 (29)	Haydn tells Leopold Mozart, visiting Vienna, that Wolfgang is the greatest composer who ever lived. Wolfgang begins collaboration with da Ponte, becomes friendly with English musical colony in Vienna.	*Haydn* quartets completed; more great piano concertos (K. 466, 467, 482); *Marriage of Figaro* begun.
1786 (30)	*Figaro* produced in Vienna, but is dropped after nine performances. Third son is born and dies.	*Prague* Symphony in D (No. 38, K. 504); Piano Concerto in C (K. 503); chamber music.

| 1787 (31) | Visits Prague, which commissions him to write an opera. He responds with *Don Giovanni*, produced triumphantly there on October 29. Receives a visit from Beethoven, who has come to Vienna at age seventeen. Leopold Mozart dies on May 28 at sixty-seven. Wolfgang is appointed to a minor post as court chamber composer. A daughter is born, but dies six months later. | C major and G minor string quintets (K. 515 and 516); *Eine kleine Nachtmusik; Don Giovanni*. |
| 1788 (32) | *Don Giovanni* is a flop when performed in Vienna. Mozart writes his three greatest symphonies even as he pours out minuets and marches for social functions as part of his court duties. Van Swieten asks him to reorchestrate Handel. | Symphonies Nos. 39 in E-flat (K. 543), 40 in G minor (K. 550), 41 (*Jupiter*) in C (K. 551). |

1789 (33)	Travels to Berlin, encounters Bach's music and plays his old organ on a stopover in Leipzig. Falls deeply into debt and starts borrowing heavily. Another daughter is born and dies. *Storming of the Bastille; start of the French Revolution.*	Clarinet Quintet (K. 581); *King of Prussia* Quartet (K. 575); starts work on *Così fan tutte.*
1790 (34)	Debts pile up as Constanze continues her "cures" at Baden. Mozart visits Mainz, Mannheim, Munich and Frankfurt (where he attends the crowning of Leopold II, though not as a member of the official retinue). Fails to profit by any of these trips. *Così fan tutte* drops out of sight after ten performances. Suffers increasing bouts of poor health.	*Così fan tutte*; string quartets K. 589 and 590, also dedicated to the King of Prussia; *Coronation* Piano Concerto, K. 537; pieces for a mechanical organ (K. 594).

1791 (35)   A stranger commissions the Requiem, but he is forced to put it aside when Prague asks him to compose an opera (*La Clemenza di Tito*) for the coronation of Leopold II as King of Bohemia and Schikaneder asks for *The Magic Flute*. His son Franz Xaver Wolfgang is born. Overcome by illness and probably exhaustion, Mozart dies on December 5.

Piano Concerto No. 27 in B-flat (K. 595); *"Ave, verum corpus"*; *La Clemenza di Tito*; *The Magic Flute*; Requiem (completed by Süssmayr).

A Note on Currency Values

Throughout this book an attempt has been made to translate the currency values of Mozart's time into modern U.S. equivalents, but such figures can be only rough approximations.

I have generally followed the estimates for European currency in the year 1789 given by Will and Ariel Durant in their book *The Age of Napoleon* (1975). The Durants give the following equivalents for currency frequently mentioned by Mozart:

gulden	$5.00
ducat	$12.50
florin	$2.50
guinea	$26.25

No effort has been made to adjust these figures to reflect the fluctuations of the American dollar in recent years; to do so would be to give a wildly inflated idea of currency values in Mozart's day as measured by known prices for various commodities and services.

The figure of $5 for the gulden during the 1780s in Vienna also conforms to the table of European currency values for the year 1820 in an article "Incomes and Outgoings in the Vienna of Beethoven and Schubert" by Alice M. Hanson, in the July-October 1983 issue of *Music & Letters*. Hanson estimates the value of the gulden in 1820 at 50 cents. As a result of the Napoleonic Wars and the collapse of the Austrian financial system in 1811, the gulden fell to one-tenth of its former value between 1790 and 1820.

Acknowledgments

Dr. Johnson said that a man would turn over half a library to make one book. In somewhat the same spirit, for many years I have been reading books and articles on Mozart, many of which are directly or indirectly reflected in this endeavor of my own. Rather than trying to give a complete bibliography, I would like to cite two major works which are, in my opinion, indispensable for anyone who writes about Mozart, or, for that matter, anyone who really tries to comprehend his life and his music: Emily Anderson's three-volume set of *The Letters of Mozart and His Family*, published originally by Macmillan in London in 1938, and Otto Erich Deutsch's *Mozart: A Documentary Biography*, published by the Stanford University Press in 1965.

Similarly, while many individuals have been helpful with my researches, I would like to name three whose help has been of especial value: Marguerite Michaels, who generously provided me with much material pertaining to twentieth-century views of Mozart; Anita Goss, who indefatigably checked many of my facts and sources; and, certainly not least, Erna Schwerin, president of the Friends of Mozart, who was kind enough to read

ACKNOWLEDGMENTS

my manuscript and who, from her vast knowledge, provided a good many corrections and amplifications. Needless to say, all responsibility for any remaining errors, as well as for all interpretations and speculations regarding Mozart and his music, remains mine alone.

Index

INDEX

INDEX

INDEX

INDEX

INDEX

INDEX

INDEX

INDEX

INDEX

INDEX

About the Author

Herbert Kupferberg is an internationally recognized music critic. Former Lively Arts Editor and record columnist of the *New York Herald Tribune*, he is now a senior editor of *Parade* magazine. His previous books include *Basically Bach*; *Tanglewood*, an illustrated history of America's leading music festival; *Those Fabulous Philadelphians*; *The Mendelssohns*; and *The Book of Classical Music Lists*. He lives in Forest Hills, New York.